Whispers Of The Divine: A Soul's Journey

OrangeBooks Publication

1st Floor, Rajhans Arcade, Mall Road, Kohka, Bhilai, Chhattisgarh 490020
Website: **www.orangebooks.in**

© Copyright, 2025, Author

All rights reserved. No part of this book may be reproduced, stored in a retrieval system, or transmitted, in any form by any means, electronic, mechanical, magnetic, optical, chemical, manual, photocopying, recording or otherwise, without the prior written consent of its writer.

First Edition, 2025

ISBN: 978-93-6554-495-4

WHISPERS OF THE DIVINE

A SOUL'S JOURNEY

UNVEILING THE HIDDEN TRUTHS OF YOUR SOUL'S PATH

SYLVIA FERNANDES

OrangeBooks Publication
www.orangebooks.in

Opening The Soul Scroll
An Invocation To The Reader

This is not just a book.

This is an awakening scroll, sealed long ago in the sacred chambers of your Soul.

Each word you read is a key, unlocking what has long been forgotten.

You may hear whispers as you turn these pages…

Whispers that don't come from the outside world—

But from deep within the caverns of your being.

The whisper of a child…

    longing to be heard.

The whisper of your ancestors…

    calling you to complete what they began.

The whisper of your guides…

    nudging you to rise, to remember.

And above all,

The whisper of your Soul,

    gently saying,

"You are not lost. You were never broken. You are coming home."

As you move through this sacred journey,

You may feel sudden emotions rising—

Tears without reason,

Warmth in your chest,

Goosebumps,

The presence of something unseen but deeply known.

These are not coincidences.

These are soul signals.

Your deeper truth, gently resurfacing.

Let yourself feel.

Let yourself remember.

Let yourself be found.

For within these pages lies not just knowledge,

> but remembrance,
>
> not just words,
>
> but energy,
>
> and not just a book,
>
> but a living bridge to your soul's eternal flame.

Welcome to the Soul Scroll.

You are exactly where you were always meant to be.

An energetic initiation into Whispers- the first call to awaken your Soul's Remembrance

༄

Acknowledgements

This book is not just a creation—it is a living prayer, born of spirit, silence, tears, love, and the grace of those who walked with me through every shadow and sunrise.

To my beloved parents, Kistu and Rosaline—though no longer in the physical realm, your blessings flow through every word I write. You are the unseen roots that have held me steady, the breath behind every dream.

To Viral Manek, my mentor and the first guiding light on this path—thank you for holding the torch when I was finding my way. Your belief in me awakened the belief in myself.

To my soul companions—Vayu and Rekha, closest to my heart. You have been my strength, my vision-keepers, and my sacred reflections during the most powerful phases of this journey. This book holds your essence too.

To my cherished circle—Raviji, Bernadine, Angel Serrao, Mr. Vilas Patil, Anjali Sarkale, Advocate Haridas, Dr Om Tavri, Dr Kruti, Dr Arvind Vartak, Jyoti Patil —thank you for being part of the soul web that continues to uplift and inspire me.

To my beloved family—my sisters, brother-in-law, brother, sister-in-law, my nieces —and to my heartbeats: my husband Mateus and our children Marvic and

Milan—thank you for your love, your patience, and the sacred space you gave me to birth this work.

To my dear clients and students—your courage and transformation inspire my own. Each of you is a chapter in my heart.

To my feline companion, my gentle healer—you sat by me in silence, anchoring energies with grace and purrs. Thank you for simply being.

To my spiritual guides, divine allies, and unseen protectors, especially Nyx, the sacred goddess of the night—thank you for cradling my soul in the dark and reminding me that creation begins there.

To my incredible editor, publisher, and designer—you helped bring my vision to life with care and dedication. I am forever grateful to Orangebooks Publications and their wonderful team—thank you for your steadfast support and the heart you put into this journey. A special note of gratitude to Payal Ghosh and Preeti Shetty.

And to myself—for choosing to rise every time it felt easier to retreat. For trusting the mystery. For surrendering. This book is a celebration of that choice.

With Love Poured Into Every Page,
~ Sylvia Fernandes

Preface

This book was born not from thought, but from silence—from the quiet spaces between my breath, where the whispers of the Divine became louder than the noise of the world.

For years, I have walked alongside souls who were searching—seeking healing, understanding, clarity, and peace. Many came with deep wounds, unseen pain, questions unanswered. What I discovered in every single journey is this: the soul never gives up on us. It gently nudges, sometimes shakes, and often whispers… guiding us back to who we really are.

Whispers of the Divine is not a book filled with theories. It is a sacred offering of real stories, divine insights, and soul wisdom. It holds the essence of what I've witnessed, channelled, and experienced over decades as a spiritual healer and seeker.

This book is for you if you've ever asked, "Why am I here?"

If you've ever felt alone, yet sensed a presence walking with you.

If you've ever cried in the night and felt a subtle light begin to rise within you the next morning.

If you know you are here for something deeper—but aren't sure what it is yet.

Each chapter is a mirror, a guidepost, a reminder.

Each story holds a frequency of healing and awakening.

Each message is lovingly crafted to bring you closer to your truth.

As you read, may you pause and breathe. May you hear not just my words, but your own soul's voice between the lines. And may you come to remember that you are never alone on this path—the Divine is always whispering.

In Grace And Love

~ Sylvia Fernandes.

Foreword

By Viral Sir – My Guide And Mentor

Some souls are born with a quiet knowing… a deep inner call to serve, to heal, to lift others beyond their pain. Sylvia is one such soul.

It has been my joy and honor to witness her unfold into the spiritual teacher and healer she was always meant to be. Her path was never conventional, nor easy. Yet, she walked it with devotion, courage, and a heart wide open to the Divine.

In Whispers of the Divine, Sylvia shares not just stories and insights, but pieces of her own soul. Her words carry truth, but more importantly, they carry frequency—the kind that gently stirs something within the reader, reminding them of who they are beneath the noise.

This book is a natural extension of her energy. It doesn't preach, it invites. It doesn't instruct, it illuminates.

To all who open these pages—know that you are in the hands of someone who has walked the fires, and emerged with light in her hands. May this work guide you, awaken you, and bring you home to your own inner whispers.

With Deep Pride And Blessings

~ Viral Sir

Master From Beyond

By Marvic And Milan – My Loving Angels

As children, we often watched our mother move through life with grace, strength, and an unshakable faith in the unseen. What we didn't always understand then, we now see clearly—she wasn't just walking her own path, she was gently lighting the way for others.

Whispers of the Divine is more than a book. It is our mother's heart on paper.

Through these pages, you will discover the depth of her wisdom, the truth of her journey, and the powerful presence she brings to every soul she touches. We've witnessed her healing countless lives—not through force, but through compassion, intuition, and her unwavering connection to the Divine.

There were times when life tested her, when the path was unclear. But she always returned to her calling. And today, we feel proud—not just of what she has written, but of the life she has lived to write it.

This book is a gift to all who are searching. If you are holding it in your hands, trust that your soul led you here. Let these whispers speak to your heart as they have spoken to ours.

We Love You, Mum.

May Your Words Awaken Many.

~ Marvic And Milan

Introduction

There comes a time in every soul's journey when silence becomes louder than noise. When the chaos of the outer world drives us inward—toward the still voice that whispers, "There is more. There is purpose. There is light, even here."

This Book Was Born In One Of Those Moments.

Whispers of the Divine is not just a title—it is the truth I've lived. It is every quiet nudge I followed when logic failed me. Every tear I cried when I felt unseen. Every moment of grace that arrived just when I was ready to give up. It is a living collection of my most sacred conversations with the Divine—some channeled, some whispered into my being in moments of silence, others revealed through the lives and healing journeys of those who walked with me.

There were days I questioned everything.

Why Me? Why Now? Why This Pain?

And every time, in the space between my breath and my breakdown, the answer would arrive—not as a loud proclamation, but as a whisper. A Divine whisper. Gentle. Loving. Transformative.

This book is for the seeker, the silent warrior, the wounded healer. For the woman or man lying awake at 3 a.m., wondering if anyone sees their pain. For the ones who feel everything so deeply that the world often feels too loud. For those who've given up only to find a tiny flicker of hope still burning in the ashes.

I Wrote This For You.

Through each story and insight, I offer a part of myself—a truth I've earned, a wound I've healed, a miracle I've witnessed. You'll meet souls who overcame unbearable losses, souls who remembered who they are, and souls who didn't think they were worthy of Divine love—until they heard it, felt it, and became it.

In writing this, I have laughed. I have cried. I have gone back to moments I had buried deep in my heart. And I have emerged, again and again, with a deeper knowing: we are never alone. The Divine is always with us—in the smallest signs, in sudden synchronicities, in the warmth of a stranger's smile, in the silence that follows surrender.

To my children, Marvic and Milan, and Mateus your love has always been my anchor.

To my guide, Viral Sir—thank you for holding the torch when I couldn't see my own light.

To my family who returned to my life at the perfect time—you are a part of this journey, and always will be.

To Leonard Sir, a gentleman in every way—thank you for your steady support, quiet strength and standing by me always where there was no hope.

And to every client, friend, and Divine presence who helped shape this work—you are etched into these pages.

This is more than a book. It is a soul map.

May it guide you gently home—to the truth of who you are.

May it remind you to listen closely.

Because the whispers have always been there.

With love, grace, and infinite gratitude,

~ *Sylvia Fernandes*

Contents

Part One

The Soul Awakens 1
- What Is The Soul? 1
- The Power Of Free Will..6
- Soul's Contract And Purpose 9
- Awakening The Soul's Calling 13
- The Signs Of Soul Suffering..16
- The Role Of Past Lives In Our Journey..............................17

Part Two

The Healing Path 22
- Why Do We Face Struggles?...22
- The Healing Path – Challenges And Lessons 24
- Healing The Soul: A Journey Of Self-Discovery 28
- Soul Retrieval Healing: Reclaiming Wholeness 37
- Tools For Healing: 46
- Connecting With The Divine..56
- Embracing Divine: Messages From Beyond 60

Part Three

The Journey Within.. 63
- The Mystical Journey Of The Soul 71
- Serving The World – A Soul In Action................................87
- Living As A Soul In A Human Body.....................................96
- The Ultimate Decision 105

Part Four

The Alchemy And Alignment.. 126

   Embracing The Shadows – The Path To
   Soul Alchemy 126
   Mystical Analogy: The Phoenix And The Shadow 128
   Soul Alignment..132

Part One
The Soul Awakens

What Is The Soul?

The soul is the essence of who we are, the energy that transcends our physical body. It is the core of our existence, a divine spark within us that connects us to the universe. The soul is often perceived as the eternal part of us that holds our deepest desires, lessons, and divine purpose.

Imagine the soul as a bright light at the center of your being, unshakable and constant, no matter what happens to your body or the external world. It is timeless, ageless, and beyond the material realm.

Example:

Ravi, a 30-year-old engineer, felt disconnected and lost after the sudden death of his mother. Despite his external success, he couldn't shake the overwhelming feeling of emptiness. Through spiritual healing, he discovered that the loss of his mother had caused a deep wound in his soul, leaving him disconnected from his true self. It was only through this realization that Ravi began his healing journey.

The Soul's Purpose

Each soul enters the world with a purpose: to learn, grow, and evolve. This purpose can be related to personal development, healing, relationships, or even the collective energy of the universe. Our soul's purpose is often intertwined with our emotions, experiences, and the lessons we are meant to learn throughout our lives.

When we align ourselves with our soul's purpose, life begins to flow more easily. However, when we are disconnected from this purpose, we often feel lost, anxious, and disconnected from ourselves.

Example:

Sita, a 40-year-old teacher, had always felt the desire to help others but never truly understood why. After undergoing soul retrieval healing, she discovered that her soul's purpose was to help others realize their own potential. Her life began to align with this purpose, and she felt a deep sense of fulfillment.

The Soul's Connection To Emotions

The soul is deeply intertwined with our emotions. Every feeling, every experience, is stored within our soul, influencing our actions, thoughts, and decisions. The soul experiences both joy and pain, and these emotions leave an imprint on our being.

When we undergo emotional trauma, it can affect our soul's vibration, leading to disharmony in our life. Understanding this connection helps us begin to heal emotionally, spiritually, and physically.

Case Study

Amrita, a young woman, struggled with anxiety and depression after a traumatic childhood. She discovered that her soul was carrying the weight of unresolved emotional wounds, which had manifested as mental health struggles. Through soul healing, she was able to release the emotional baggage and start living a life of peace and joy.

The Soul's Role In Physical Healing

The soul is not just an abstract concept; it plays a crucial role in physical health. When the soul is in pain, it manifests in the body in various ways, such as illness, fatigue, or even chronic pain. The body and soul are deeply connected, and healing the soul can lead to profound physical recovery.

Example:

Vikram, a 50-year-old man, had suffered from chronic back pain for years, with no medical explanation. After exploring soul healing, he realized that the pain was a manifestation of unresolved emotional wounds from his childhood. After healing these wounds, his physical pain diminished significantly.

Soul's First Steps

Entering The World – Birth And Early Years

Have you ever looked into the eyes of a newborn and sensed something ancient? That's the soul—wise, luminous, and timeless—entering the human experience once again.

When I was a child, I often felt like I didn't belong. I couldn't explain it then, but I carried a silent knowing, a sense of something bigger than the world around me. Many of us do. We arrive here with sacred memories, yet we are wrapped in forgetfulness, as if life gently places a veil over our soul's true identity. This is not a punishment—it is part of the journey.

Why Do We Forget Who We Truly Are?

The forgetting is essential. Imagine watching a movie when you already know the ending—it loses its magic. In the same way, the soul forgets so it can remember. The thrill of rediscovering who we truly are is the heartbeat of our human life.

But this forgetting is not easy. As children, we are like open receivers—absorbing every emotion, energy, and belief around us. The soul is still fresh from the divine realm, and yet, it must quickly adapt to the density of Earth. The love we receive—or don't—becomes our first teacher.

Case Study 1: The Sensitive Child Who Shut Down

Netra, now in her 40s, came to me during a soul healing session. As a child, she was labeled "too emotional." Her family valued logic and success, not feelings. She would sense energies, dream vividly, and often talk about angels. But her father dismissed it as imagination. Slowly, Netra shut that part of her down. She became successful, but disconnected from her spirit. Through soul healing, we uncovered that her sensitivity was her soul gift. Once embraced, she began intuitive painting—

and soon found not only joy but financial freedom through her soul-aligned art.

The Role Of Family, Environment & Culture

We choose our families. Yes, even the difficult ones. They are our first mirrors, our first soul contracts. The environment we grow up in plants the seeds of our beliefs—about love, money, fear, safety, and power.

In my case, I grew up in a household where emotions were often silenced. Expressing my feelings wasn't welcomed. For years, I believed being spiritual meant being quiet and invisible. I didn't know that this suppression was shaping my soul's first wound—the fear of being seen. Later, this would become the very wound I'd need to heal so I could step into my soul's purpose.

Case Study 2: The Warrior Born Into Silence

Raj, a healer in his 50s, always felt different. His family was steeped in generational trauma. Rage and silence were the only languages spoken. He coped by becoming the 'fixer'—never speaking about his own pain. In his 30s, a tragic divorce cracked him open. During Akashic healing, we traced his soul's path through lifetimes of silence. He had taken vows to not speak out. Once released, he began to use his voice—first through poetry, then through public speaking, sharing stories of healing for men who never felt seen.

Culture As A Framework, Not A Cage

Culture shapes us, but it must not limit us. What you were told about who you are may not be the full truth.

You are more than your gender, religion, nationality, or class. Your soul came to Break some patterns, not just repeat them.

Reflection Questions:

1. What was your earliest memory of feeling 'different' or misunderstood?

2. What messages did your family or culture give you about being "too much" or "not enough"?

3. What wound from childhood still feels unhealed?

The Power Of Free Will

From the moment our soul incarnates into a human form, it steps into a world of duality—light and shadow, choice and consequence, fate and freedom. While we may enter life with a divine blueprint—a soul contract—there remains one extraordinary gift granted to every human: free will.

Free will is the sacred power to choose. It is the silent force behind every thought we think, every path we walk, and every lesson we embrace or resist. It is not just a mental faculty but a divine tool that determines how we experience our soul journey. With free will, we can create, destroy, heal, hurt, love, or withdraw. It is where destiny and desire collide.

But why is free will so powerful?

Because it holds the key to transformation.

Because it allows the soul to evolve.

Imagine life as a vast landscape—your soul came with a map, perhaps even a compass. But how you walk the terrain, which turns you take, how often you pause, fall, rise again—that is entirely up to your free will.

The Paradox Of Choice

Many believe that if we have a soul plan, everything is predestined. But free will exists within the framework of our destiny. It is the soul's way of navigating karma, learning lessons, and discovering who we are at our core.

You may be destined to meet a soulmate—but whether you open your heart to them is your choice.

You may be called to serve—but whether you accept the calling is up to you.

You may be gifted with healing—but whether you use that gift or deny it is your decision.

My Journey With Free Will

In my own path, I have faced many forks in the road. There were times I turned away from divine nudges because of pride, fear, or simply exhaustion. I ignored signs, denied my gifts, resisted healing—and each choice shaped me, not as punishment, but as part of my awakening.

The choices I made during the darkest times—especially when I felt like a beggar, humiliated, unsupported—were my most sacred teachers. Every "no" to the Divine led me to the edge. And yet, it was the conscious "yes"—the moment I chose to listen, to surrender, to heal—that opened the floodgates of grace.

Free will was never about perfection; it was about presence.

About choosing from the soul, not from fear.

About saying yes to our higher self, even when the ego screams no.

A Moment Of Reflection

Think about your own life for a moment.

What choices have defined you?

Where have you felt pulled by fate, yet resisted by fear?

What happens when you choose from love, not lack?

The power of free will lies in your ability to realign at any moment. You are never too far gone. You are never too late. The path may wind, but your soul always knows the way.

Case Study: Rewriting Destiny Through Choice

Anaya came to me feeling hopeless. A series of toxic relationships had drained her emotionally and financially. She believed her fate was sealed—doomed to be abandoned, unloved, and used.

In our Akashic session, her records revealed a soul pattern of abandonment going back several lifetimes. This life was her chance to break that pattern—not by waiting for someone to rescue her, but by choosing herself.

During our work together, Anaya was given the option to walk away from her current relationship, but it meant losing financial security. She hesitated. Her logical mind said no. But her soul whispered yes.

She chose yes.

That moment of choosing from free will, not fear, cracked her open.

She moved into her own space.

Started her healing practice (a soul gift long buried).

And within months, she met someone who saw her fully—because she finally saw herself.

Her soul contract offered the opportunity for freedom. But it was her free will that activated the shift.

In the next section, we'll explore the soul's contract and how free will dances with destiny to create the masterpiece of your life.

Soul's Contract And Purpose

"Before I formed you in the womb, I knew you." – Jeremiah 1:5.

The Sacred Blueprint: Did We Choose This Life Before Birth?

Yes. You did.

In the infinite stillness before time began for you, your soul sat in a sacred council—bathed in divine light—and whispered a "yes" to this life. Not for punishment. Not by chance. But for purpose.

You chose your parents, your location, your gifts, and even your trials. You knew the path might burn you, but it would also awaken you.

Like the seed that must crack open to become a tree, your soul chose this cracking, because it knew what it was destined to become.

Soul Agreements: The People We Meet

Every soul that crosses your path is part of a web woven long before your first breath.

Some come to love you.

Some come to break you.

Some come to mirror the pieces you must remember.

These are Soul Agreements—spiritual contracts made before birth. Your mother who never hugged you. The friend who stood by you in your darkest night. The child who left too soon. None of it is random.

Shalini, a healer from Delhi, couldn't understand why her closest friend cheated her in business. Through soul contract work, she discovered their connection from a past life where she had abandoned him in war. This life, his betrayal wasn't revenge—it was a wake-up call for her to value herself, her intuition, and her boundaries. That pain was sacred curriculum.

Divine Assignment: Discovering Life Purpose

Your purpose is not a job. It is the essence that flows through everything you do. It may express as healing, teaching, nurturing, creating, leading, or simply being light.

Some people awaken to it early. Others need breakdowns, losses, and miracles.

My Awakening

In 2017, I stood at the crossroads—financially broken, emotionally betrayed, and spiritually drained. My divine teacher, Shri Viral Manek, appeared as the guide soul I had once chosen. Through Divya Shakti, my path began to light up. The pain? It was preparation. The rejection? Redirection. And today, I stand as a Medium for many—living my purpose, healing souls, and transforming karmic patterns.

The Soul Council – Our Pre-Birth Planning Room

Before incarnating, we meet with our spiritual guides, guardian beings, and other souls we will interact with. This is where we choose the life we're about to enter—based on what our soul wants to learn, release, or master.

Why? So that our soul's curriculum unfolds with divine timing.

"Even your greatest enemy in this lifetime might have once held your hand and said, 'I'll play the villain, so you can awaken to your light.'"

The Veil Of Forgetting – Why We Don't Remember

If we remembered everything from the start, there would be no free will, no curiosity, no journey. The Veil is not punishment, it's a sacred fog—to help us rediscover who we are, not be told.

This forgetting allows us to grow through experience, not just knowledge.

Trigger Soul's Vs Healing Souls – The Catalysts And Comforters

Some people shake us awake (trigger souls), while others soothe our wounds (healing souls). Both are essential.

Your ex who betrayed you? A trigger soul meant to teach self-worth.

Your best friend who always understands? A healing soul who walks beside you.

They agreed to play their roles before you even met.

Rewriting Contracts – Can We Change Our Fate?

Yes. While soul contracts are pre-agreed, they are not fixed forever. Through healing, forgiveness, awareness, and higher consciousness, we can:

* Release outdated agreements
* Clear karmic cords
* Shift timelines
* Invoke new soul companions

Your soul evolves, and so can your

Final Soul Whisper

Nothing in your life has been a mistake.

Every heartbreak, every joy, every detour—was written by the hand of your soul.

Your job isn't to figure it all out.

Your job is to remember, trust, and realign with that higher script you once authored in love.

Awakening The Soul's Calling

(The Sacred Moment You Remember Who You Truly Are)

There comes a moment in every soul's journey when the world as we know it begins to shimmer — not with glamour, but with a mysterious, sacred invitation. It's subtle at first — a tug in the heart, a question that won't go away, a deep ache for something… more. This is the awakening of the soul's calling — a turning point, where life is no longer just about survival, but about meaning, essence, and truth.

To awaken is not to add something new to yourself; it is to remember what you already are — an eternal being, with divine intelligence and purpose, temporarily experiencing a human life.

What Is A Soul Calling?

Your soul's calling is the unique frequency of your divine purpose — that thing you were born to offer, to be, to express. It often feels like a deep, quiet fire burning inside, even when the world around you doesn't see it. It may not always make sense logically, but it feels profoundly right.

You might have ignored it for years, or silenced it with duty, fear, or distractions. Yet it waits patiently — until one day… it can't be ignored anymore.

When Does This Awakening Happen?

For some, it comes in a moment of joy. For others, it's birthed from deep loss, heartbreak, or illness. You might be walking down a busy street and suddenly feel you don't belong — not in a sad way, but as if your soul is whispering: "There is more. Come home."

This awakening isn't loud. It is sacred. It demands your attention, presence, and courage. It begins when:

You realize you are more than your body, more than your name, job, or roles.

You start receiving signs — repeated numbers, strange coincidences, or dreams.

You hear an inner voice guiding you, softer than thought, but stronger than doubt.

Reflection Exercise: Whisper Of The Soull – Are You Truly Listening?

Take a moment for yourself.

Find a quiet space where you feel safe, undisturbed.

Sit comfortably.

Close your eyes and gently place your hand over your heart.

Breathe in deeply… hold… and exhale slowly.

Let each breath draw you inward.

Now, in this space of stillness, ask your soul…

1. "Have You Been Calling Out To Me?"

Think back — was there a moment, a fleeting second, where something deep inside whispered to you?

A nudge... a dream... a repeated sign you couldn't explain?

Write about it. Explore it. Even if it doesn't make sense.

2. "What Signs Have I Missed?"

Look back at the synchronicities — the repeated numbers, symbols, dreams, words spoken by strangers that felt too personal.

Could it be the Universe trying to reach you?

Make a list. No matter how small or silly they may seem.

3. "What Have I Been Too Afraid To Listen To?"

Sometimes the soul whispers things we don't want to hear — truths that would change our lives.

What is the truth you keep burying?

What would happen if you listened to it?

4. "If I Let Go Of Fear, What Would I Become?"

Imagine yourself fearless. Imagine you woke up tomorrow with full clarity of your purpose.

Who would you be? What would you do?

Write a page beginning with: "If I wasn't afraid, I would..."

Bonus Practice: The Soul's Mirror

Stand before a mirror. Look deep into your own eyes.

Say out loud:

"I am listening. I am ready. Guide me to my purpose."

Let tears come if they must.

This is not just an exercise. This is the beginning of remembrance.

The Signs Of Soul Suffering

What Does Soul Suffering Look Like?

Soul suffering is not always loud; it doesn't shout. It whispers in the quietest moments, and sometimes, it's so subtle that we miss it. But if you listen carefully, you'll hear it — like a deep sigh from the depths of your being, a cry for help that's been stifled for too long.

Soul suffering feels like drowning in your own skin, as though you're trapped in a life that isn't truly yours. It's the aching emptiness that sits in your chest when you look in the mirror and no longer recognize the person staring back at you. It's the exhaustion that no amount of sleep can heal, because your heart is tired, your spirit is tired. And you've been carrying this burden for so long that you don't know where it ends and you begin.

You walk through life, smiling, laughing, doing what's expected of you. But inside, you're screaming, yet the world cannot hear you.

Example:

Rahul, a 45-year-old father, always appeared strong to his family, his friends, his colleagues. But when he was alone, he was empty. His soul had been carrying the pain of decades — years of unhealed wounds from childhood, a failed marriage, and the constant pressure of being the "rock" everyone depended on. Despite his outward successes, Rahul had never healed the invisible scars he carried. His heart was broken, but he continued to walk with a smile. He didn't know that, with every painful event, his soul was quietly breaking apart. He was carrying it all — alone, until one day, it became too much. His body began to ache, his spirit, broken.

This is the silent cry of the soul, the suffering that people often carry without even realizing it.

The Role Of Past Lives In Our Journey

As we walk the path of life, we often find ourselves asking, "Why am I going through this? Why does it feel like certain struggles keep reappearing?" These questions echo within us, pointing to a deeper mystery— the idea that the answers to some of our challenges may not lie only in this lifetime. What if there is more to our story, a thread that runs through many lifetimes, shaping the patterns and experiences we face today? This thread is known as our past lives.

The belief in past lives can be challenging for many, especially when it is not part of the traditions they were raised in. For instance, many Western religions, such as Christianity, do not directly support the concept of reincarnation. Yet, when we look deeper, there are subtle hints in the sacred texts that suggest the possibility of a soul's journey across lifetimes. Just as the Bhagavad Gita speaks of the eternal soul, the Bible, too, offers glimpses of this deeper understanding.

The Soul's Eternal Journey: A Glimpse In The Bible

Though reincarnation isn't explicitly mentioned in the Bible, certain verses point to the idea of life beyond this one. In John 9:1-3, when Jesus encounters a man blind from birth, His disciples ask, "Who sinned, this man or his parents, that he was born blind?" Jesus responds that neither sinned, but the man's condition is a result of divine purpose. This verse suggests a continuity of the soul, pointing to a journey that extends beyond one life, where actions from previous lives could influence the present.

Additionally, Matthew 17:10-13 refers to John the Baptist as Elijah returned, which could be interpreted as a reference to reincarnation. These glimpses in the Bible may not be as direct as those in the Bhagavad Gita or other spiritual texts, but they hint at a deeper understanding of the soul's journey—one that transcends a single lifetime.

The Bhagavad Gita And The Soul's Immortality

In the Bhagavad Gita, Lord Krishna speaks directly to the concept of the soul's immortality and its journey through many lifetimes. In Chapter 2, Verse 20, Krishna explains, "For the soul, there is neither birth nor death at any time. It is not slain when the body is slain." The soul, as Krishna says, is eternal and unchanging. It passes through many cycles of birth and death, each time taking on a new body, a new life, but always carrying the essence of its past experiences.

This profound teaching aligns with the understanding of reincarnation, where the soul learns, grows, and evolves through successive lifetimes, refining itself with each experience. Every lifetime, every incarnation, brings the soul closer to enlightenment, each filled with lessons that shape who we are and who we are becoming.

The Quran And The Eternal Nature Of The Soul

In the Quran, while the concept of reincarnation is not explicitly stated, there is a recognition of life after death and the eternal nature of the soul. The Quran emphasizes that the soul will return to its Creator and be judged based on the deeds of the life it lived. Surah Al-Qiyama (75:36-40) speaks of the soul's resurrection, and it hints at the soul's journey, not confined to one physical existence but extending into eternity. The eternal journey of the soul, facing rewards or consequences based on its actions, suggests that there is continuity beyond this lifetime.

The Unseen Journey: Understanding The Influence Of Past Lives

Whether we believe in past lives or not, one undeniable truth is that the challenges we face in this life often feel like they come from deeper, unexplained sources. Have you ever wondered why you may have an intense fear, an unshakable pattern, or an inexplicable connection to someone you've never met before? These experiences may be echoes of past lives, unresolved karmic imprints that continue to influence our journey in this lifetime.

Our soul is a reservoir of memories, lessons, and experiences accumulated across lifetimes. These experiences shape our emotions, our actions, and our choices. The feelings of guilt, grief, anger, or even profound love that we carry are often linked to actions or relationships from past incarnations. We may not always be consciously aware of them, but they live within us, shaping the course of our lives.

The Soul And Karma

The concept of karma teaches that our actions, thoughts, and emotions create a ripple effect in our lives and in the lives of others. The soul carries these karmic lessons from past lives, and they influence our current life experiences. Understanding the soul's karma allows us to release negative patterns and heal from past wounds.

When we are able to forgive and heal from past karma, we free ourselves from the chains of the past and create space for a more fulfilling present and future.

Case Study:

Neelam, a woman in her 30s, had a repeating pattern of toxic relationships. Through soul retrieval and past life regression, she discovered that her soul was carrying unresolved karma from a past life where she had been betrayed by a loved one. Once she healed this past life wound, her present relationships began to transform.

Chapter Conclusion

In this chapter, we've explored the soul's essence, purpose, and connection to our emotions and physical health. The soul is an eternal part of who we are, and it holds the key to our true purpose in life. Healing the soul is an essential step in creating harmony and alignment in our lives, leading to a more peaceful and fulfilled existence.

As you continue through the book, keep in mind that every part of this journey is interconnected. Understanding your soul's path is the first step in healing, and it will guide you towards a deeper connection with yourself and the divine.

Part Two
The Healing Path

Why Do We Face Struggles?

Struggles are not random accidents in life. They are intentional experiences chosen by the soul before birth as part of its evolutionary journey. We face struggles because our soul is here to grow, evolve, and return to its divine nature—and this growth often happens through contrast, discomfort, and challenge.

Here Are The Key Reasons Why We Face Struggles:

1. Soul Contracts And Karmic Patterns

Before incarnating, the soul creates contracts with other souls—agreements to help each other grow. These often show up as painful relationships, betrayals, or loss. They're not punishments but soul-designed scenarios to teach us forgiveness, compassion, strength, or boundaries.

For example a soul may choose parents who are emotionally unavailable to learn self-reliance and unconditional love.

2. Breaking Old Cycles

We repeat patterns across lifetimes until we learn the lesson. Struggles are often the soul's way of pointing us to a pattern we must finally release.

If you keep attracting the same kind of toxic relationships, or financial losses, your soul is saying:

"Pause. Reflect. Change the inner belief creating this reality."

3. Awakening Inner Power

Struggles challenge the false self—the ego—and awaken the true self. When everything external falls apart, we're forced to go within. This is when our inner healer, warrior, creator, or mystic is born.

Think of the butterfly. It must wrestle inside the cocoon to strengthen its wings. If you cut the cocoon open early, it cannot fly. In the same way, your struggle gives you spiritual muscle.

4. Expanding Consciousness Through Experience

We don't learn by reading about pain or joy—we grow by living it. The soul seeks direct experience. Through pain, we learn empathy. Through joy, we learn gratitude. These lived emotions expand consciousness.

Struggles break the illusion that we are separate from the divine. They often become the doorway to faith, surrender, and deeper truth.

5. Redirection Toward Your Soul Purpose

Struggles often redirect us to our true path. A job loss may push you toward your soul calling. A failed relationship may lead to deep self-love. What feels like an end is often a divine redirection.

The Gift Within Every Struggle

Every struggle carries within it a seed of awakening. If watered with awareness and healing, it blooms into wisdom.

When you ask, "Why me?" the deeper truth is:

Because your soul is ready.

Ready to heal.

Ready to grow.

Ready to remember who you truly are.

The Healing Path – Challenges And Lessons

Healing is not just a process—it is a sacred journey. A journey that takes us deep into the core of our being, unearthing the pain, patterns, and programming that have held us back across lifetimes. But why is healing required in the first place?

Every soul carries imprints—memories, wounds, and karmic residues from this life and others. These imprints manifest as emotional blocks, repeating patterns, physical ailments, or relationship struggles. Healing is the act of bringing light to these shadows. It is the soul's way of cleansing and realigning with its true divine essence.

Challenges show up on our path not as punishment, but as divine assignments—each one carrying a lesson. When we view challenges through the lens of healing, we understand that they are messengers, not enemies. They come to reveal something hidden within us that needs awareness, forgiveness, or transformation.

The real power of healing lies in the lessons we learn through each experience. As we grow through pain, loss, or confusion, we gain conscious awareness—the inner light that helps us navigate future paths with wisdom.

Every lesson integrated is a step toward spiritual maturity. And with each step, we begin to recognize the patterns we once fell into. This awareness becomes our protection—a divine armor that helps us avoid repeating the same mistakes.

Healing is not about perfection. It is about progression. It is about learning to walk with compassion for ourselves and others, while listening to the soul's whispers that guide us gently back to the truth.

So, when the next challenge appears, ask:

What is this trying to teach me?

What is the soul trying to heal through this experience?

Because once the lesson is embraced, the challenge dissolves—and in its place, a new level of consciousness emerges.

The Soul's Growth Through Pain And Joy

The journey of the soul is not linear—it is expansive, spiral, and deeply transformative. While we often celebrate moments of joy, it is through the dual forces of pain and joy that the soul truly evolves. Both are essential teachers, guiding us toward wholeness.

Pain: The Cracked Door To Awakening

Pain is not the enemy—it is the soul's alarm bell, waking us up from unconscious living. It forces us to stop, reflect, and go inward. When life is comfortable, we rarely question our beliefs or choices. But pain shatters the illusion of control and invites us to explore the deeper layers of our being.

Pain Teaches Us To:

Let go of attachments that no longer serve us

Face buried emotions or traumas

Build resilience and emotional maturity

Rely on divine strength rather than external support

Pain is often the sacred fire that burns away illusions, leaving behind the purified truth of who we are.

Joy: The Light Of The Soul's Expansion

While pain breaks us open, joy is the soul's natural state. It arises when we are in alignment with our truth—when we create, love, serve, and connect deeply with ourselves and others.

Joy is not just about pleasure—it is the deep inner glow that comes from:

Living authentically

Expressing our gifts

Experiencing divine connection

Feeling gratitude and wonder

When we allow ourselves to fully feel joy, we expand our vibration and become magnetic to abundance, love, and clarity. Joy is not the absence of problems—it is the presence of purpose and connection.

How Both Pain And Joy Work Together

Pain pushes us.

Joy pulls us.

Pain reveals what needs to be healed.

Joy reveals what needs to be celebrated.

They are two sides of the same coin—each essential to the soul's growth.

Example1: Meera's Dark Night And Breakthrough

Meera was a spiritual seeker who seemed to have everything—family, career, a stable life. Yet, an unexpected diagnosis shattered her world. Her body weakened, but her spiritual senses opened. In her stillness, she began hearing divine messages, seeing visions, and reconnecting with her past lives. What she thought was the worst time of her life became her awakening into healing work.

Pain was the gateway to her soul's real calling.

Example 2: Samir's Joyful Leap Of Faith

Samir, a banker by profession, always loved music but never pursued it. One day, after attending a spiritual retreat, he followed an inner nudge and began singing at small events. The joy he felt was indescribable—a soul joy that filled his life with purpose. Slowly, he transitioned to a healing career using music as therapy.

Joy was the compass that led him back to his soul's voice.

Integrating The Dual Wisdom

As souls, we are not meant to chase only joy or avoid pain. We are meant to integrate the wisdom of both.

Ask yourself:

What has pain taught me that nothing else could?

What brings me soul-level joy, and how can I embrace more of it?

When you walk the path of healing, both your tears and your laughter are sacred. The soul remembers each as part of its divine unfolding.

Healing The Soul: A Journey Of Self-Discovery

Healing The Soul

"You are not broken. You are becoming whole."

What Does It Mean To Heal The Soul?

Soul healing is not about fixing something damaged. It is about remembering. Remembering who you truly are beyond the pain, beyond the roles you play, beyond the wounds of your past.

It's the return to wholeness — when the soul sheds the layers of fear, grief, betrayal, shame, abandonment... and reclaims its original divine light.

Sometimes, we seek healing.

Sometimes, healing finds us — through loss, heartbreak, illness, or spiritual awakening.

But either way, the soul never gives up.

It whispers, cries, screams... until you listen.

How Does Soul Healing Happen?

Soul healing is layered and multi-dimensional.

It can happen through:

Energy work (like aura cleansing, chakra balancing, space clearing)

Emotional release (crying, journaling, therapy, forgiveness rituals)

Spiritual alignment (prayer, chanting, connecting with your guides, soul retrieval)

Creative expression (art, music, dance, writing — where your soul gets to breathe)

Silent stillness (meditation, nature walks, presence)

It is not linear. You may feel healed one day and triggered the next. That's okay. Healing is circular — like spirals — revisiting the same wounds at deeper levels, but each time with more wisdom.

What Kind Of Circumstances Lead To Soul Healing

Often, the soul is awakened into healing when life throws us into the fire:

A sudden loss or breakup

Repeated patterns (like abandonment or rejection)

Chronic illness or unexplained fatigue

Feeling lost, empty, or disconnected from your purpose

Nightmares, insomnia, or anxiety

Intuitive nudges that something feels "off" despite everything looking okay

These are not punishments. These are soul alarms — calling you back to yourself.

When Should One Begin Healing?

The moment you feel a disconnect between who you are and who you were born to be, is the time to start.

Some start young.

Some start after decades.

Some start after loss, some after love.

But it's never too early or too late.

Your soul has perfect timing.

Start When:

You feel the pain outweighs your joy.

You're tired of repeating the same emotional cycles.

You feel a yearning for more meaning.

You're spiritually curious or seeking divine connection.

Who Can Do Soul Healing

You Can.

Everyone has the innate power to heal themselves, especially with the right tools, guides, or facilitators.

But when the pain feels too deep, you may feel lost or stuck. That's when a soul healer can help — someone trained in intuitive, energetic, or spiritual modalities who can:

Read your energy and aura

Connect with your soul guides

Retrieve lost soul fragments

Cleanse ancestral or karmic blocks

Hold sacred space for your transformation

You don't need to be perfect to begin.

You just need to be willing.

My Example

There were moments when I had everything — the image, the knowledge, the titles — and yet I felt shattered inside. Despite helping others, I felt I was screaming into the void of my own emptiness. Finances dipped, trust was broken, and support vanished.

The Divine didn't abandon me. It waited.

It waited for me to stop fighting and start listening.

It wasn't dramatic. It was simple. A tear in meditation. A strange dream. A cat curling beside me when I couldn't get out of bed.

And I knew... the healing had begun.

Closing Thought

Healing the soul isn't about changing who you are.

It's about coming home to your essence.

The you that is whole, divine, radiant —

Healing Emotional Wounds

"The deepest wounds are the ones no one sees... yet they ask for the loudest healing."

What Are Emotional Wounds?

Emotional wounds are the imprints of pain we carry in our energy field — from childhood trauma, betrayal, rejection, abandonment, humiliation, loss, or feeling unloved.

They may not bleed... but they echo:

In your fear of intimacy

In your inability to trust

In the repeated patterns of self-sabotage

In the way you push people away before they can leave

In that silent inner critic that tells you, "You're not enough."

These wounds create an invisible wall between your soul and the life you're meant to live.

Why Must These Wounds Be Healed?

Because when wounds stay unhealed, they become filters — you stop seeing the world as it is, and start seeing it through pain.

They block abundance, relationships, health, and most importantly, your connection with the Divine.

Healing emotional wounds is like cleaning a foggy mirror — so your soul's brilliance can finally reflect back to you.

The Power Of Forgiveness And Letting Go

Forgiveness is not condoning what happened.

It is choosing peace over poison.

Letting go is not forgetting.

It is remembering with love, instead of pain.

Forgiveness is one of the most sacred medicines in soul healing — not for others, but for your own freedom.

My Own Healing Through Forgiveness

There was someone in my life I trusted deeply — both spiritually and emotionally. But they hurt me in ways that shook my foundation. For years, I carried that wound like a hidden thorn. I smiled. I helped others. But inside, I was bleeding.

Then one night, in a quiet moment of prayer, the voice of my soul whispered:

"You don't have to carry this anymore."

I cried.

Not because I was weak.

But because my soul was finally ready to release.

I wrote them a letter I never sent.

I forgave them not because they asked for it…

But because I deserved peace.

That forgiveness didn't make me forget.

It made me whole.

How To Begin Healing Emotional Wounds

1. Acknowledge The Pain.
Don't suppress or spiritualize it. Say it: "Yes, I was hurt. Yes, this matters."

2. Feel It Safely.
Allow yourself to cry, write, express. Feelings are the soul's language.

3. Understand The Lesson.
What was this teaching you? Maybe it was about boundaries, self-worth, or unconditional love.

4. Forgive — At Your Own Pace.
You don't need to rush. But you do need to choose eventually. Choose to set yourself free.

5. Let Go With Grace.
Burn the letter. Release the memory in a ritual. Imagine cutting energetic cords. Watch yourself rise lighter.

A Reflection For The Reader:

Have you ever held on to pain because it felt safer than letting go?

Are you ready to release that story now?

Can you open your heart to the freedom of forgiveness?

The Ultimate Result: Reconnecting With Your True Self

When we carry emotional wounds, we become fragments of ourselves. We live from fear, not faith. From reaction, not intention. From protection, not purpose.

But healing — deep, soul healing — is not just about "feeling better."

It is about remembering who you truly are beneath the pain.

You are not your trauma.

You are not your abandonment.

You are not the betrayal.

You are a Divine being, temporarily wrapped in human form, here to live, love, and serve.

Case Study: Rekha's Journey Back To Herself

Rekha, a client in her 40s, came to me completely disconnected from life. She had a good job, a loving child, but felt numb. Her relationships were transactional, her days mechanical. She said:

"I don't know who I am anymore... I'm just surviving."

In our sessions, we uncovered a core wound from childhood — her mother constantly criticized her and withheld affection. Rekha internalized the belief that love must be earned, and perfection was the price.

Over time, I used Aura Healing to clear the pain she carried in her energetic field. I also worked through forgiveness letters, inner child meditation, and mirror work.

One Day She Called And Said:
"I looked in the mirror today… and for the first time, I saw me. I felt like I've come home to someone I lost long ago — myself."

That was it.

No fireworks. No applause.

Just sacred reconnection.

Her voice changed. Her posture shifted. Her energy softened.

She started painting again. Laughing again. She said she felt alive. Whole.

In Simple Words:
When we heal… we don't become someone new.

We simply return to the truth of who we are.

The one that was always there — just waiting under the wounds.

End Note: Healing The Soul

Healing the soul is not a destination — it is a sacred remembering.

We are not broken; we are simply carrying experiences that veil our truth.

Through courage, compassion, and divine grace, we release the pain, forgive the past, and slowly return home — to the radiant, whole, and powerful soul we have always been.

Every tear, every breakthrough, every moment of surrender is a step back into our light.

And in that light...

We rediscover peace, purpose, and the true meaning of love.

Soul Retrieval Healing: Reclaiming Wholeness

Healing isn't just a word—it's a journey. A sacred journey of rediscovery, of reconnecting with the parts of ourselves we've lost over time. It's not about becoming something new—it's about becoming whole again.

From the first cry of birth to the last breath of our human journey, we experience countless moments of pain, joy, and sorrow. These moments imprint upon us, leaving invisible marks on our souls. It could be a moment of rejection as a child, a betrayal in a relationship, or the sudden loss of a loved one. With each painful event, a piece of our soul seems to fade away, lost in the shadow of emotional trauma.

Soul loss doesn't discriminate. It touches everyone, from the innocent child to the elderly, from the powerful to the powerless. It's as though, with every painful moment, our soul gets chipped away, leaving behind pieces scattered in the wind, longing to be found again.

Imagine a child whose innocent laughter is overshadowed by constant scolding or neglect. Every harsh word, every ignored cry, is a wound on the soul. Over time, the child starts to feel disconnected, lost, as though they don't belong in this world. Their laughter dims, and a piece of their soul is left behind.

Consider an elderly person who has lived a life full of sacrifice, only to be left alone in their later years. Their children have moved away, their friends have passed on, and they're left feeling like a shadow of the vibrant person they once were. The joy that once filled their heart has faded, and they, too, have lost pieces of their soul to isolation and loneliness.

But just like the broken pieces of a puzzle, these lost fragments can be found and restored.

Soul retrieval healing is the sacred process of reclaiming those lost fragments and reuniting them with the whole. Through gentle healing practices, we can reach out to those lost parts of ourselves—those fragmented pieces—and bring them back to their rightful place.

For The Child:

When a child's soul is fragmented due to neglect or emotional trauma, soul retrieval can restore their sense of self-worth and joy. I recall a case of little Aarav, a 7-

year-old who had been emotionally abandoned by his parents. His parents were physically present, but their emotional absence created a gap in his soul. His laughter was shallow, his eyes lacked the sparkle of innocence. Through a process of guided healing, we called back the fragmented parts of Aarav's soul, and slowly but surely, he started to smile again. His parents saw a transformation in him—he was more connected, more joyful, and felt loved once again.

For The Elderly:

When an elderly soul has been neglected or forgotten, it often feels like a deep ache in their heart. Take the example of Mrs. Rao, an 82-year-old woman who had lived a life of service to her family. However, as her children grew up and moved away, she felt abandoned. The void left her feeling disconnected, her soul longing for the companionship and love she once had. In her healing session, we were able to retrieve the fragments of her soul that had been lost in the loneliness of her later years. Through gentle soul retrieval, Mrs. Rao felt a renewed sense of purpose and love. Her children, too, noticed the change, as she began to embrace the love they had for her.

For Adults And Young Adults:

Soul loss isn't just something for children and the elderly; it affects everyone. Consider the young professional who's lost in the fast-paced world of work, constantly chasing success at the expense of their emotional well-being. Or the adult who's suffered from childhood trauma, the memories of which still haunt them. They often walk through life feeling disconnected, as though something is missing. Through soul retrieval, these individuals can reclaim the energy and vitality that was once theirs. The lost fragments of their soul are brought back, and with them comes a renewed sense of purpose, peace and fulfillment.

One such example is Rhea, a 34-year-old woman who had been emotionally scarred from an abusive relationship. The weight of her past held her back from moving forward. She sought help, and through soul retrieval, we were able to reconnect her with the lost fragments of her soul. She felt a deep sense of relief, as though a weight had been lifted off her heart. The healing process allowed her to forgive herself, regain her sense of self-worth, and step into a new chapter of her life, one filled with hope and self-love.

Healing For All Walks Of Life:
Whether you're a child, an elderly person, or an adult caught in the chaos of life, soul retrieval healing is for everyone. It's for the broken-hearted, the forgotten, and the lost. It's for those who feel incomplete, those who can't seem to find their way.

This sacred process is a reminder that no matter how lost you feel, there is always a way back to wholeness. Your soul has never left you. It is always there, waiting for you to call it back, to embrace the pieces that have been scattered along the way.

The journey of soul retrieval is a process of self-love, self-compassion, and deep transformation. It's about acknowledging the pain, the suffering, and the loss, and giving yourself permission to heal. It's about letting go of the past, welcoming the present, and allowing your soul to be whole again.

This chapter emphasizes how soul retrieval healing applies to everyone—regardless of age or life circumstances—and offers a deep emotional connection with the reader. It's meant to touch the heart and help them understand the sacredness of their soul's journey.

Soul's Healing Through Energy And Aura

In the vast tapestry of existence, every living being is intertwined with an invisible thread of energy. This energy forms the very fabric of our soul's essence. Our aura—an ethereal, glowing field that surrounds our bodies—acts as a mirror to our inner self, reflecting the balance (or imbalance) within. It is through this radiant field that the soul communicates, expressing its truths, its pain, and its growth.

The Spectrum Of Energy And Aura

Our auras are not static. They shimmer, vibrate, and change, adapting to the shifts in our emotions, thoughts, and even the very energies we encounter from the external world. Just as the soul carries the story of our past, present, and future, the aura reveals these tales—woven in an intricate dance of colors, each representing different emotions, states of mind, and energetic imprints.

The colors of the aura are deeply telling. For example, a brilliant yellow aura may suggest joy, intellect, and clarity, while a muddled gray or black hue could signify grief, confusion, or deep-rooted negative energies that need healing. Each hue—red, blue, green, violet—tells the story of the soul's current state. When these colors become dull or clouded, they indicate that something deeper within the soul needs attention.

The Defects In Our Aura

As we live through life, our soul picks up emotional, physical, and spiritual wounds. These wounds manifest as defects in our aura. Leaks, tears, scars, and psychic cords can create cracks in the aura, letting out the very energy we need to nourish ourselves, leaving us feeling drained, confused, or disconnected from our divine purpose. These defects can be the result of trauma, unresolved emotional pain, past life experiences, or toxic relationships.

Consider the story of Radhika, a woman in her late thirties. Radhika had been carrying the weight of abandonment from childhood, a wound so deep that it had cast a shadow over her entire life. The abandonment created a significant tear in her aura, affecting her sense of self-worth and leaving her energetically unbalanced. She was unable to trust or form deep connections with others, always afraid that they too would leave her. After undergoing aura healing, her aura was cleared of the deep scars left by this trauma, and she was able to begin trusting herself and others again. Her life shifted as she healed from the inside out, and the tear in her aura was no longer a barrier to her happiness.

These energy disturbances can also take the form of psychic cords—connections formed with others that drain our energy. These cords often arise from toxic or codependent relationships. The more attached we are to someone energetically, the stronger these cords become, sapping our vitality and blocking our soul's full potential.

The Healing Of The Aura: Restoring Balance

Restoring balance to our aura requires a deep understanding of energy. Through energy healing, we can clear the imbalances and re-align the frequencies of the aura, allowing the soul to heal. This is not a passive process. It requires conscious intention, focus, and the willingness to release old patterns that no longer serve our highest good.

When we heal the aura, we are not just healing the physical body. We are healing the soul—the seat of all emotions, experiences, and memories. The process involves reconnecting with the divine energies, aligning ourselves with higher frequencies, and tapping into the flow of universal love and light.

Healing the aura also involves chakra balancing—aligning the nine main energy centers of the body with the frequencies of light and love. When our chakras are open and balanced, energy flows freely, and we experience vitality, clarity, and spiritual alignment. However, when one or more chakras become blocked or out of balance, it affects the flow of energy in our body and disrupts our connection to the divine.

Take the example of Ajay, a young man who came to me with constant feelings of fatigue, confusion, and emotional instability. His aura was clouded with dense energy from past heartbreaks and unresolved emotional trauma. His heart chakra, which governs love and emotional well-being, was blocked. Through energy healing and chakra clearing, Ajay was able to release old patterns, and his aura was restored to a vibrant, harmonious state. He felt lighter, clearer, and more connected to his divine essence.

The Frequency Of The Soul

At its core, everything is energy, vibrating at a certain frequency. Our thoughts, emotions, and beliefs create frequencies that shape our reality. When we vibrate at a high frequency, we attract positivity, abundance, and spiritual growth. But when we carry lower frequencies—such as fear, guilt, shame, or anger—we create a dense energetic field that prevents us from stepping into our full potential.

Healing through energy and aura work is about raising our frequency—aligning with the divine flow of light and love. As we elevate our frequency, we begin to experience the world in a more positive, expansive way. We attract higher vibrations into our lives and start to manifest our soul's desires with ease.

Practical Healing Techniques For Aura Cleansing

The path to healing is one of awareness, intention, and action. Here are a few practices that can help you begin healing your aura:

1. Smudging with Sage or Palo Santo: Burn sage or Palo Santo and allow the smoke to wash over your body, clearing away negative energies and refreshing your aura.

2. Visualization: Close your eyes and visualize a brilliant light surrounding you. Imagine this light cleansing and healing every layer of your aura. See any negativity being released into the light, transmuted into positive energy.

3. Crystals: Crystals such as Amethyst, Selenite, and Rose Quartz are powerful tools for aura healing. Place them around your body, meditate with them, or simply carry them with you to restore balance and harmony.

4. Cord Cutting: Often, we form energetic attachments with people, places, or situations that no longer serve our highest good. These psychic cords can drain our energy and keep us tethered to negative emotions and past experiences. By performing cord cutting, you can sever these attachments, freeing your energy and allowing you to step into your true power. This can be done through visualization, prayer, or with the help of a healer. When you cut these cords, it frees both you and the other person from the energetic ties that bind you, allowing for healing and personal growth.

5. Chakra Meditation: Focus on each chakra, one by one, and visualize each energy center being filled with bright, healing light. Allow the light to expand, clearing away blockages and restoring the flow of energy.

By embracing the power of energy healing and aura work, you can begin to transform not only your life but the lives of those around you. The soul is a divine entity, capable of profound healing, and the aura is the key to unlocking its true potential.

Tools For Healing:

Meditation, Crystals, Oils, Candles, Affirmations And, Angelic Healing.

In the previous chapter, we explored how divine guidance speaks to us and how our souls are often caught in the grip of external pressures, resisting the truth of who we truly are. As we embrace that guidance, it's important to remember that healing and spiritual alignment don't simply come through intellectual understanding. True transformation requires us to engage not just our minds, but also our body, emotions, and spirit.

This is where the tools for healing come into play. Meditation, crystals, oils, candles, affirmations, and angelic healing are all sacred instruments that help us ground divine wisdom into our daily lives. They act as bridges, guiding us from intellectual awareness to tangible transformation. Each tool supports our journey, helping us clear blockages, align with our highest self, and open the door to deeper connection with the divine.

These tools work in harmony with our soul's purpose, assisting us in navigating the challenges of life while remaining aligned with our divine blueprint. They help us tune into our highest potential and live in greater peace, clarity, and abundance. In this chapter, we will explore each of these tools, giving you practical ways to incorporate them into your life, ensuring that they are not just concepts but living practices that support you in your healing journey.

Meditation: The Gateway To Divine Connection

Meditation is one of the most powerful tools to connect with the divine. By quieting the mind and focusing our awareness inward, we open the channel through which divine guidance flows. This practice not only calms our nerves but helps us move past the limitations of our logical thinking, allowing us to access deeper, intuitive knowledge that transcends the intellectual mind.

In meditation, we cultivate a stillness that invites the soul's voice to be heard, offering clarity, peace, and a profound sense of connection to the divine. When we regularly practice meditation, we align ourselves with the natural flow of life, allowing divine wisdom to guide us and lead us toward healing.

Crystals: The Earth's Healing Vibrations

Crystals carry powerful healing energies that help us align with higher frequencies. The vibrations of crystals can assist in clearing blockages, restoring balance, and enhancing our spiritual practices. Each crystal holds its unique energy signature, supporting specific aspects of our lives such as healing, abundance, and spiritual growth.

When we work with crystals, we tap into the wisdom of the earth and the universe, allowing them to guide us toward healing. These energetic allies help us realign with our divine essence, bringing peace, healing, and clarity.

Essential Oils Aromatherapy For The Soul

Essential oils are not only soothing fragrances but are powerful allies in healing. They have the ability to influence our emotions, calm our nervous system, and uplift our energy. Different oils carry different frequencies, which can help us release negativity and promote a state of balance and harmony.

By using oils such as lavender for relaxation, frankincense for spiritual connection, or lemon for clarity, we invite the energetic properties of nature to support our healing journey.

Aromatherapy becomes a sacred ritual, where we allow the divine power of plants to guide and nurture us.

Candles: The Light Of Transformation

Candles are symbols of divine light and transformation. The flame represents the balance between light and shadow, and by lighting a candle, we invite the presence of the divine into our space. Each candle color carries a specific energetic vibration that supports different intentions, such as healing, love, or abundance.

When we light a candle, we invoke a shift in our energy, creating a sacred atmosphere that allows us to connect more deeply with our higher self and divine guidance. It's a simple, yet powerful, tool that can help illuminate our path toward healing and divine alignment.

Affirmations: Aligning With Divine Truth

Affirmations are powerful tools that help us align our thoughts and beliefs with our highest potential. When we speak words of truth, we reprogram our subconscious mind, releasing limiting beliefs and replacing them with empowering ones. Affirmations create an energetic alignment with divine wisdom, helping us manifest the life we desire.

When we use affirmations, we are actively speaking the truth of our soul, declaring our worth, power, and divine connection. This practice helps us overcome fear and self-doubt, empowering us to step into our divine potential.

Angelic Healing: Calling Upon Divine Messengers

Angelic healing is an ancient and profound tool for healing. Angels, as divine messengers, are always present, ready to guide, protect, and heal us. By invoking the angels, we invite their assistance in our healing journey, allowing them to carry our prayers, lift our burdens, and provide the guidance we need.

Each angel holds specific attributes that correspond to different healing needs. For example: Archangel Michael offers protection and helps release fear and negativity.

Archangel Raphael is the angel of healing, supporting physical, emotional, and spiritual.

Archangel Gabriel aids in communication, creativity, and clarity.

Archangel Uriel brings wisdom, insight, and illumination during times of confusion or darkness.

When we call upon these angels, we open ourselves to their divine assistance. They help us align with our higher selves and clear the energetic blockages that may be hindering our progress. Their presence is a powerful tool for healing, as they bring peace, comfort, and divine intervention into our lives.

Other Healing Tools To Consider:

Sound Healing (Sound Baths, Singing Bowls, Tuning Forks): Sound vibrations have the power to shift our energetic frequencies, clearing blockages and promoting healing on a cellular level.

Smudging (Sage, Palo Santo, or Incense): Smudging is an ancient practice used to clear negative energy from spaces, objects, and individuals, creating an environment of peace and positive energy.

Visualization and Guided Imagery: Using mental imagery to envision healing light or a connection with divine beings helps to shift our consciousness and create lasting transformations.

Sacred Objects (Talismans, Amulets, Statues, Scapulars): Objects that hold spiritual significance can serve as reminders of divine protection, abundance, or other qualities you wish to manifest in your life.

Sigil, Mandalas, yantras also helps in healing.

Nature Walks (Earthing or Grounding): Spending time in nature and connecting with the earth's energy can help restore balance, heal emotional wounds, and align us with the rhythm of the universe.

Planetary Alignments: Harnessing Cosmic Energies For Soul Growth

Our souls are not only connected to the earth but also to the vast cosmos. The movements of the planets can significantly influence our personal energy and spiritual growth. By understanding the planetary alignments and their effects, we can tap into the cosmic flow that aids our soul's journey.

Each planet has a unique energy that governs different aspects of our lives. For example, Mercury affects communication, Venus influences love and relationships, Mars governs action and strength, and Saturn teaches us lessons of discipline and patience. By aligning our actions and intentions with favorable planetary alignments, we can enhance our spiritual growth and make the most of the energies available to us.

You can use astrology to understand which planetary transits are most favorable for specific areas of your life, or simply meditate during powerful planetary alignments (such as during a full moon or a retrograde) to receive clarity and healing.

Inner Child Healing: Reconnecting With Your Innocence

Our soul's journey is often deeply affected by the wounds of our inner child. These wounds, caused by past traumas or unmet needs, can block us from stepping into our full potential.

Inner child healing is the process of reconnecting with the pure, innocent aspect of ourselves and nurturing the parts that were hurt or abandoned.

To heal your inner child, take time to reflect on your past and acknowledge the emotional scars. Use meditation to visualize comforting your younger self, offering love, reassurance, and healing. By doing so, you release old emotional patterns that prevent you from fully experiencing life's joy and freedom.

Womb Healing: Releasing Energetic Blocks From The Source Of Creation

The womb is not only a physical space where life begins, but it also holds deep spiritual significance. Womb healing helps to release negative energies, traumas, and blockages that may have originated in this space, whether from past life experiences, ancestral trauma, or personal events.

By focusing on the womb during meditation and using healing practices like sound therapy or gentle breathwork, you can clear any stagnant or painful energies that may have been carried throughout your life. This healing fosters a deeper connection with your feminine energy, creativity, and the ability to manifest your desires with ease.

Space Healing: Clearing And Aligning Your Environment

Our physical environment has a profound impact on our energy and soul's journey. Whether it's the clutter in our home, the energy of our workplace, or the spaces we inhabit, they all influence how we feel and how aligned we are with our soul.

Space healing involves clearing out negative energy, organizing your environment, and ensuring that it supports your soul's journey. Use tools such as smudging with sage, sound baths, or crystals to cleanse the energy of your space. As you create a harmonious environment, your own energy will begin to shift, supporting your spiritual alignment and growth.

Forgivenesss: Liberating The Soul From The Past Hurts

Forgiveness is one of the most powerful tools for soul alignment. Holding onto grudges or resentment creates energetic blockages that prevent the flow of love, peace, and joy. By practicing forgiveness, we release ourselves from the chains of the past and allow our soul to heal.

Forgiveness doesn't mean condoning harmful behavior or forgetting the pain—it means freeing yourself from its grip. Take time to reflect on any unresolved anger or resentment you may be holding, and offer forgiveness to yourself and others. Through this practice, you release the old energy and make space for healing and growth.

Compassion: Opening The Heart To Universal Love

Compassion is the ability to feel and act with kindness and empathy toward yourself and others. It is essential for soul alignment, as it allows us to transcend the ego's judgments and open our hearts to the divine essence that exists in all beings.

Start by practicing self-compassion—acknowledge your own struggles and offer yourself the same kindness you would extend to a loved one. Then, extend this compassion to others, recognizing that we are all on unique journeys. As you embrace compassion, you align your energy with unconditional love, which is the essence of the soul.

Gratitude: Acknowledging The Divine Gifts In Every Moment

Gratitude is a powerful tool that shifts your energy and aligns you with your soul's purpose. By focusing on the blessings in your life, you open the door for more abundance, love, and peace to flow into your experience.

Take time each day to express gratitude for the little things—your health, your relationships, your experiences. Even in difficult times, look for the lessons and blessings that are present. Gratitude cultivates an attitude of receptivity, allowing your soul to align with the flow of divine energy and abundance.

Love: The Highest Frequency Of The Soul

Love is the most profound remedy for soul alignment. It is the frequency at which the soul vibrates when it is in its purest form. When we operate from a place of love—both for ourselves and others—we connect with the essence of who we are and the divine presence within.

Cultivate love in your life by practicing self-love, embracing forgiveness, and extending kindness to all living beings. As you live in alignment with love, your soul will feel lighter, your energy will expand, and your path will be illuminated with grace.

Conclusion: Embracing Practical Remedies For Soul Alignment

The tools and remedies discussed in this chapter serve as a bridge to reconnect with your soul. By aligning with the universal energies of nature, healing past wounds, and living with intention and purpose, you create a life that is in harmony with your soul's true essence. Every practice, whether it's meditation, planetary alignment, forgiveness, or love, is a step closer to experiencing the divine flow of life and fulfilling your soul's purpose.

As you implement these remedies, remember that the path of soul alignment is a journey, not a destination. Trust in the process and be patient with yourself as you heal and grow. Every step you take towards alignment brings you closer to the peace, joy, and fulfillment that your soul yearns for. Live in union with your soul, and witness the transformation not only within yourself but also in the world around you.

Healing is an ongoing process, and these tools are companions along the way. Use them regularly to stay connected to your divine essence and to create a space for transformation.

With each step you take, trust that you are being guided, protected, and supported by divine forces, and know that the healing you seek is always within reach.

Connecting With The Divine

In today's chaotic world, many of us lose sight of the most essential aspect of our existence—the connection with the Divine. Our lives are often filled with noise—material pursuits, social distractions, and the constant rush of daily life. In this whirlwind, we begin to focus on things that do not serve our higher purpose: anger, jealousy, hatred, and the temptation to meddle in other people's lives. Instead of being centered in the Divine, we get entangled in distractions that take us further away from the spiritual essence we are meant to embrace.

We live in an age where, often, more attention is given to the material world than to the energy that guides and sustains us. We spend our days in conflict—whether with others or within ourselves—and find it increasingly difficult to find peace. Instead of nurturing our spiritual connection, we waste energy on negativity and comparison, often failing to recognize the immense blessings the Divine has already bestowed upon us.

But there is hope. The Divine is always present, waiting for us to turn inward, away from the chaos, and reconnect. When we do so, we begin to realize that true happiness does not come from external achievements or validation. It comes from an internal alignment with the Divine energy that flows through us.

The Spiritual Path Amidst Life's Chaos

Connecting with the Divine is not a complex or far-off process. It is not something that requires us to detach completely from the world or retreat from our responsibilities. It is about finding balance—learning to navigate through the chaos of life while remaining rooted in the spirit of the Divine. When we immerse ourselves in spiritual practices such as meditation, prayer, or simply being present, we align our thoughts, emotions, and actions with the Divine energy that connects us all.

The distractions we face—whether they are feelings of anger, jealousy, or simply being caught up in the drama of others—are all part of the human condition. But we have the power to rise above them. The more we allow ourselves to focus on negativity and external judgments, the further we drift from the peaceful, balanced state that is our birthright. Instead, if we can bring our attention back to our soul's essence, we can begin to see life with a new perspective—one rooted in spirituality, gratitude, and love.

Finding Peace Through Divine Connection

The key to healing is to recognize that we are not at the mercy of our external circumstances. Our soul is an eternal being, and it is not influenced by petty arguments, material gains, or the judgment of others. These things may seem important in the moment, but they are transient. True peace and healing come when we cultivate our connection with the Divine.

When we learn to focus on what truly matters—love, compassion, and divine purpose—we create an internal harmony that cannot be disturbed by the turbulence of life. By working with the SPIRIT of the Divine, we begin to transcend the lower energies of anger, jealousy, and hatred. We recognize that these emotions only hold us back, and by letting go of them, we make room for the pure Divine energy to heal and uplift us.

It is essential to remember that we are all divinely blessed. Each of us has been given unique gifts and opportunities. But how often do we take these blessings for granted? How many times do we focus on what we lack instead of appreciating what we have? In our rush to seek more, we forget to be grateful for the abundance that is already present in our lives.

Gratitude: The Key To Spiritual Connection

Gratitude is one of the most powerful tools we have in reconnecting with the Divine. When we express gratitude, we open ourselves to receiving more blessings from the universe. Gratitude shifts our focus from what is missing to what is already present, allowing us to see the Divine hand in every aspect of our lives.

The act of simply being thankful for the life we have can transform our entire perspective. When we express gratitude for the blessings in our lives, we invite more of that energy into our being. This is how we begin to heal our soul—by recognizing and embracing the gifts the Divine has already given us.

A Story Of Transformation: Rajiv's Shift In Focus

Rajiv was a successful entrepreneur who had built a lucrative business from the ground up. On the outside, his life appeared perfect—money, status, and respect. However, Rajiv was constantly dissatisfied. He envied others who seemed to have it all together, often comparing himself to them. He spent his days looking for ways to gain more success, more recognition, and more material possessions.

His focus was entirely on external achievements, and it left him feeling empty inside. He became consumed by anger and frustration, unable to appreciate the abundance in his life. The more he sought external validation, the more he felt disconnected from his true self.

One day, after a long period of emotional turmoil, Rajiv attended a spiritual retreat. He was introduced to the practice of gratitude. At first, he resisted, feeling that it was too simple. But as he began to practice daily gratitude—acknowledging the blessings he had in his life—something shifted. His perspective began to change. He started to see his life through the lens of abundance rather than scarcity. Instead of focusing on what he didn't have, he began to appreciate everything he had.

Rajiv's transformation was profound. He stopped comparing himself to others, found peace in his own accomplishments, and embraced the divine blessings that had always been present. His soul began to heal, and he found a new sense of purpose in his life—one that was aligned with the divine energy that had always been guiding him.

Returning To Balance: The Spiritual Practice

To reconnect with the Divine, we must first quiet the noise that surrounds us. Life is loud and demanding, but in the stillness, the Divine speaks. Whether through meditation, prayer, or simply being present in nature, we must create space in our lives to listen. By doing so, we allow ourselves to become aligned with our higher purpose.

Let go of anger, jealousy, and the compulsion to control everything around you. Instead, allow yourself to be guided by the Divine energy that exists within you. When we focus on our spiritual journey, we begin to align our emotions, thoughts, and actions with the universal flow of energy, bringing balance and healing to our lives.

The Divine is not distant. It is within us, surrounding us, guiding us. It is through this connection that we can transcend the chaos, heal our souls, and live lives full of gratitude, peace, and alignment with our highest purpose

Embracing Divine: Messages From Beyond

There comes a point in our lives when we must stop and listen. Listen to the whispers of our soul, the subtle messages from beyond, urging us to make a change, take a leap, or free ourselves from the chains of fear and doubt. Yet, so many of us ignore this inner guidance. We believe ourselves too clever, too logical to be led by something as intangible as intuition or divine messages. We rely on our minds, trusting in our own ability to navigate life, often overlooking the wisdom that lies deeper within us.

We've all encountered moments when things feel off, when something just doesn't sit right with us, but we push it aside. "It'll be fine," we tell ourselves, or, "I can handle this." And so, we continue to walk the path that seems right in front of us, ignoring the subtle whispers of divine guidance that could lead us to peace, to freedom, to true happiness.

Take, for instance, the story of Shivani. A highly educated woman, successful in her career and earning more than her husband, she found herself trapped in a toxic relationship. Her husband, though capable of sharing life's joys, spent her earnings on his family, never allowing her the freedom to live for herself. Despite her strength and accomplishments, Shivani remained confined by his controlling ways, her spirit slowly eroding under the weight of neglect and restriction.

This behavior, this relentless adherence to toxic patterns, does more than rob us of joy—it wounds our very soul. When we choose to ignore the divine guidance that whispers of freedom and fulfillment, we inflict deep scars on our inner being. Our soul, the eternal spark of who we truly are, suffers in silence, its purpose obscured by the pain of unhealed betrayals and stifled dreams. Every act of self-denial, every moment we sacrifice our true calling for the sake of conformity, chips away at the brilliance of our soul. In doing so, we stray further from our destined path and lose sight of the divine potential that yearns to be expressed. Our soul's cry for liberation grows louder with each unheeded message, reminding us that true healing begins when we align our actions with the eternal wisdom within.

The message from beyond is clear. It is time to listen. It is time to let go of the logical mind that tells us we can handle everything ourselves and open ourselves up to the possibility that the universe is guiding us toward something greater, something more fulfilling, something that will bring us peace.

Are you ready to embrace that divine guidance? Are you willing to step out of the prison of your own mind and trust that there is a higher plan for you, waiting to unfold? Or will you continue to hold onto the chains of a life that is no longer serving you, too proud or too scared to take the leap into the unknown?

The Choice Is Yours.

Part Three
The Journey Within

"Your sacred space is where you can find yourself again and again."

~ Joseph Campbell

The journey within is not marked on any map, nor can it be walked with physical feet. It begins in the stillness — in a moment of pause, when the outer world goes silent and your soul whispers, "There is more." That whisper is the invitation. That is where it all begins.

How To Start

You don't need the perfect setting, a monastery, or a retreat. You start where you are — with a willingness to look within. The first step is honesty. To ask yourself:

Who am I beneath my roles, expectations, and wounds?

Often, pain or discontent becomes the catalyst. A loss, a betrayal, or even an existential void — something breaks through the surface and urges you to seek deeper meaning. That moment is sacred. It's your soul knocking, saying "Come home to me."

Our Destination

The destination is not a fixed place — it is a state of being. Peace. Wholeness. Alignment. It is coming back to your essence, free of illusions and full of divine remembrance. It's the place where you no longer search for love, worth, or purpose — because you know you already are all three.

Obstacles Along the Way

Like any sacred pilgrimage, this inward journey is strewn with challenges:

Old traumas and emotional baggage resurface.

Self-doubt and fear whisper lies.

Ego resists, trying to keep control.

The outer world distracts.

But remember, every obstacle is a gatekeeper to your deeper truth. They are not punishments, but portals.

How To Decide The Path

There's no single path inward. Meditation, journaling, silence, healing work, sacred scriptures, intuitive guidance, or simply being in nature — all can be paths.

The key is presence. The heart knows. The soul remembers.

Ask yourself often:

"What feels like truth, not comfort?"

"What awakens my soul, not just pleases my mind?"

What Do We Need to Carry

Travel light. Let go of judgment, expectations, the need for perfection.

Carry Instead:

Self-compassion — it's your shield.

Curiosity — it keeps the light on.

Willingness to feel — that's your compass.

Faith — in your own soul and the Divine's timing.

Criteria For Success

This is not a race, and there is no finish line.

But you'll know you're deep in the journey when:

You begin to respond rather than react.

Peace replaces anxiety, even if the outer world is chaotic.

You start honoring your intuition over validation.

Love — for yourself, others, and life — becomes your natural state.

A Real-Life Reflection

Take for example Radhika, who lost her husband unexpectedly and felt shattered. But instead of escaping the grief, she allowed it to speak to her. In her silent nights, she journaled, cried, prayed, and questioned everything. Slowly, she felt a presence— her own soul— guiding her. Today, she teaches others about resilience and divine connection. Her grief became the gate through which her soul walked into light.

Raising Your Energy: Walking The Path Of Light

Raising Your Energy And Vibrations

Raising your energy isn't just about feeling good — it's about returning to your original frequency of truth, love, and divine essence. When the soul is burdened by fear, shame, guilt, or attachment, it vibrates lower. But as we heal and realign, the frequency naturally rises.

Ways To Raise Your Vibrations:

Inner Stillness – Meditate, breathe consciously. Silence amplifies soul whispers.

Authentic Expression – Speak your truth. Suppressed emotions lower energy.

Gratitude – This isn't cliché — gratitude instantly shifts your field.

Nature – It recalibrates your auric field and grounds the soul.

Chanting & Sound – Mantras, music, or tuning forks realign your vibration.

Service – When you uplift another, you multiply your light.

Outer World Impact

The outer world constantly interacts with our field. Crowded spaces, harsh words, media, or even the company we keep can either uplift or drain us.

Protective Practices:

Cleanse your aura daily (smudging, salt water, violet flame, etc.).

Be mindful of your environment and energetic hygiene.

Discern who gets access to your sacred energy.

Use energy shields or simple affirmations like:

"Only love and truth may enter my field."

Pitfalls On The Path

The journey upward is beautiful — but not without its traps. Sometimes we unknowingly fall into spiritual bypassing or ego traps:

Avoiding Emotions: Thinking "high vibration" means ignoring pain.

Truth: Real growth is feeling and transmuting, not escaping.

Superiority Complex: Feeling more "evolved" than others.

Truth: True light is humble. The soul doesn't compare.

Chasing Light, Avoiding Shadow: Only seeking bliss.

Truth: Wholeness is embracing all — joy, fear, wounds, and wonder.

A Soulful Reminder

Energy is not about being positive all the time — it's about being real, honest, and anchored in your truth. Your vibration rises when you stop pretending, when you love yourself in the darkness, and when you walk with courage even while trembling.

The Power Of Thoughts: Gatekeepers Of The Soul

Our thoughts are not just fleeting whispers in the mind— they are commands to the universe. Each thought creates a ripple in our energy field, which in turn attracts experiences, people, and outcomes. When left unchecked, thoughts rooted in fear, scarcity, or unworthiness become unconscious programs— dictating our reality from the shadows.

"You don't see the world as it is. You see it as you think it is."

Why It Matters On The Inward Journey

When you begin the journey within, your thoughts become louder — as if the soul is holding up a mirror. Old narratives resurface: "I'm not good enough," "I'll always be alone," "Nothing works out for me."

These thoughts are not you — they are echoes of past wounds, inherited beliefs, and karmic imprints asking to be witnessed and rewritten.

Real-Life Case Study: Shivani's Transformation

Shivani, a 45-year-old teacher, constantly battled anxiety and money blocks. She'd done healing work but nothing seemed to "stick." During a session, we traced her recurring thought: "I don't deserve ease."

It stemmed from her childhood, where love came only when she worked hard or sacrificed herself. This one thought was commanding her entire life — attracting hardship, missed payments, and exhaustion.

Once she identified and reframed this belief to "Ease is my natural state. I deserve to be supported by the universe," — her body relaxed. Within a month, she received unexpected financial support, new job offers, and most importantly, a sense of calm she had never known.

Soul Exercise: Relieving And Reliving

"From Thought to Truth" Ritual

Step 1: Conscious Capture

Write down 3 recurring negative thoughts that visit you often. Be raw.

Step 2: Inner Inquiry

For each, ask: Where did this come from? Is this really mine? How old is this thought?

Step 3: The Soul Rewrite

Now, close your eyes, place a hand on your heart, and speak out a new truth that your soul wants to affirm.

Example:

Old thought: "I'm always alone."

Soul truth: "I am deeply connected to myself and held by the Divine."

Step 4: Relive With The New Thought

Visualize a past moment where this negative thought hurt you. Now replay it — but insert your new soul truth.

Let your body feel the shift. Breathe into it.

End with: "It is safe to believe differently now."

Closing Reflection

When you heal your thoughts, you rewrite the story your soul has been trying to retell for lifetimes.

Your mind is not the enemy — it is the portal. Guide it with love, and it becomes the bridge between your wounded self and your divine self.

Thoughts As Portals – Rewriting The Soul's Dialogue

In the sacred journey within, our thoughts are not just mental chatter — they are the architects of our reality and the gatekeepers of our soul's evolution. This chapter delves into the magnetic power of thought, revealing how each belief, conscious or unconscious, either expands or limits our spiritual path.

We explore the emotional weight of inherited thoughts, how they silently shape our frequency, and how healing begins by identifying and transforming them. Through real-life stories like Shivani's, we witness how a single thought can either anchor us in suffering or liberate us into flow.

Using a guided soul exercise, you will begin to relieve past burdens and relive your life through the lens of truth. This practice opens a gateway to self-love, clarity, and energetic alignment.

Ultimately, this chapter is an invitation to reclaim authorship of your inner narrative — to realize that your soul is not your story, but your storyteller, longing to create a new tale of grace, ease, and divine power.

The Mystical Journey Of The Soul

There comes a time when silence speaks louder than words.

When the wind carries messages no one else can hear,

And a mirror no longer reflects the face…

But the light behind the eyes.

This is the beginning.

Not in a temple. Not at a retreat. Not even in a spiritual classroom.

But in the hush of a breakdown, in the shiver of a dream, in the sudden knowing that "this world is not all there is."

This is the moment the soul stirs.

The Whisper and the Pull.

The mystical journey begins subtly. Almost unnoticeably.

A scent of something sacred in the ordinary…

A stranger's words feeling like they were meant only for you…

Numbers repeating. Animals appearing. A feather in your path.

No logic can explain it. And yet… your heart remembers.

It is not a memory of this life,

But of a vow made in the ethers long ago —

"I will awaken when the time comes… And I will return to Light."

The Call Behind The Curtain

Life begins to shift.

You no longer feel at home in crowds.

Your favorite foods lose flavor.

The success that once thrilled you feels empty.

The laugh you once wore now feels like a mask.

You begin to ask:

Who am I?

Why am I really here?

What is it I am meant to do… before I leave?

This ache is not sadness.

It is the echo of the soul wanting to be born again —

Not in body, but in purpose.

The Path Of Initiation

Every mystic must walk alone at first.

The mystical journey often begins with a Dark Night of the Soul.

You may lose everything — money, love, health, reputation…

Not as a punishment, but as a sacred stripping away.

You are being undone to be remade.

Here, illusions fall.

Attachments break.

Your ego trembles.

But the soul begins to glow in this fertile void.

You hear songs in silence.

You see symbols in clouds.

You talk to stars.

You begin to feel… something or someone is guiding you.

And you are right.

The Companions In Disguise

The soul sends messengers — not always angels.

Sometimes your deepest healing comes through the one who breaks your heart.

Sometimes your biggest awakening comes from betrayal.

The illness, the rejection, the loss — they were coded into your path

by your own soul before you were born.

Pain isn't the enemy. It is a sacred locksmith.

It opens the ancient door

that you sealed long ago

when this journey first began.

The Mystical Gateways

At some point, you begin to remember past lives.

A place you've never visited feels like home.

A language you've never learned stirs emotions.

A name calls to you in your dreams.

You start to travel dimensions in meditation.

You walk with ancestors.

You see colors that don't exist on Earth.

You speak to trees and feel them listening.

You are crossing into the realm of the soul mystic.

Meeting the Inner Oracle.

Now, you are no longer seeking God in the sky.

You are no longer running to gurus.

You sit beneath your own soul's tree.

And she speaks.

She may take the form of any divine being, of a white owl, of an ancient grandmother.

She may appear as a child version of you.

Or she may be light itself — pure, pulsing, breathing love.

She tells you:

"You were never lost.

You were only asleep."

The Suspense Of The Unknown

You don't know what comes next.

You may wake up one day and feel called to move to another city.

You may feel a divine pull to leave your job, end a relationship, or build something the world has never seen.

You may lose friends. You may be misunderstood.
But you are no longer guided by approval.
You are guided by Truth.

And with that comes a strange confidence —
not of the mind, but of the eternal knowing that
"I am not this name, this body, this story."

And Still… the Journey Goes On

You are still human.
You will still cry.
You will still doubt.

But now, you walk with Grace.
Your tears become sacred waters.
Your laughter, a healing vibration.
Your hands… instruments of Light.

You are no longer just living.
You are weaving.

Each word, thought, and touch now has frequency.

You don't speak. You bless.

You don't work. You offer.

You don't try. You allow.

This is the mystical soul journey.

A Soulful Example: THE BLIND DREAMER

A woman named Leora was born blind.

From childhood, she said she could see colors with her heart.

She would sit and draw — not with eyes, but with memory.

When asked how, she'd say, "My soul remembers Light."

Doctors dismissed her visions.

Family pitied her.

But she grew… and began painting.

At 35, her artwork was displayed — filled with colors she had never physically seen.

At 40, a mystic visited and told her:

"You were a color-keeper in Lemuria. You came back to paint Heaven on Earth."

Leora cried... not because she was sad — but because, finally, someone remembered her soul's contract.

That day, she stopped calling herself blind.

She said,

"I am sighted in the soul. That is enough."

The Path Of Sacred Remembrance

Close your eyes. Breathe deeply.

Say softly:

"I now call back the parts of me that remember.

I open the gates to my soul's library.

I am ready to walk the mystical path with trust,

Even if the road is not lit.

For I carry the Light within me."

Wait. Listen.

The soul will answer.

Gifted Initiation: "The Soulfire Unveiling

A Sacred Opening into the Temple Within

A Message to the Reader

In a world where initiations often require journeys to distant mountains, weeks of silence, or thousands spent on ceremonies under the stars...

Here, in this moment, in this page...

you are being initiated—freely, fully, mystically.

No outer temple.

No robe.

No chant.

Just your presence.

Because the true altar has always been within you.

And this is your moment to remember it.

Why This Is A Gift

This initiation does not demand a passport.

It does not ask you to be perfect.

It does not want anything in return.

It is the cosmic embrace your soul has longed for—

A chance to pause… breathe… and step fully into your sacred remembering.

Your soul said yes long ago.

This page is just catching up.

The Ceremony Of The "Soulfire Unveiling"

1. Sit in stillness

Turn off the world. Let silence bathe you.

2. Place your right hand on your heart, and your left on your womb or navel.

This is the bridge between the realms—Spirit and Earth.

3. Whisper Aloud:

"I receive the Soulfire Unveiling.

I accept the divine truth of who I am.

I awaken the memory of my essence,

My power, my path, and my eternal light.

I am now reconnected."

4. Let Whatever Comes… Come.

Tears. Visions. Goosebumps. Peace.

They are all your soul's way of welcoming you back.

Symbols of the Initiated

After this sacred moment, don't be surprised if:

You feel different in your body.

Your voice feels deeper.

You start hearing whispers of intuition more clearly.

Animals behave differently around you.

You begin to dream with vivid symbolism.

You recognize a spiritual family member in a stranger's eyes.

This is not fantasy.

This is the unveiling of your soulfire.

Why This Matters

Dear Soul Reader,

Most people live their entire lives outside themselves,

Chasing love, validation, and meaning in things that fade.

But you—you said yes to a journey inward.

To meet your soul, hold it, and walk with it.

That's not small.

That's sacred.

You have received a celestial gift, wrapped not in paper… but in divine light.

It will continue to unfold in dreams, signs, synchronicities.

You didn't just read a book.

You walked through a Stargate.

Walking with the Soulfire

Living as an Initiate of the Inner Light

Opening Quote: "The soul does not awaken in thunder; it unfurls in silence. What you carry now is not just fire, it is remembrance."

The Flame Has Been Lit From the moment you received the Soulfire Unveiling, a subtle shift occurred. You may not have seen it—but your soul did. You stepped into your sacred remembrance. Now, the question is not "What did I receive?" but "How do I live this?" This chapter offers you the path forward.

1. Daily Soul Touchstones

Your soul does not need grand acts. It seeks simple presence. These daily rituals allow your inner light to stay steady:

Morning Soul Check-In:

Hand on heart, eyes still closed, whisper: "How may I serve my soul today?"

Soul Scripting:

Each morning, write a paragraph from your soul. Don't think. Flow. The truth will surprise you.

Nature Walks (Barefoot if Possible):

The Earth is a conductor. It heals your body while recharging your soul frequency.

Soul Name Whispering:

Some of you may have received a soul name during the initiation. Whisper it daily. Let it echo through your energy field.

2. Sanctuary Of Silence

In a world of noise, the soul speaks in silence.

Create a weekly Sanctuary Hour—no screens, no sound. Just you, a candle, and your breath.

In This Space:

Your past lives may speak.

A forgotten gift may return.

A divine message may unfold.

Do not expect. Just listen.

3. Serving Through Soulfire

Service does not always look like action. It looks like presence.

Let Your Flame Serve:

By listening when someone is breaking

By blessing even when others curse

By showing up with peace where others panic

Your frequency becomes your offering.

4. The Soulfire Codes

These are codes received during the transmission of the Soulfire. Speak them aloud. Let them anchor within.

I do not betray my soul for comfort.

I shine, even when others dim.

I bless, not blame.

I rest without guilt.

I serve without self-loss.

I remember who I am.

You may write these on mirrors, walls, or carry them as talismans.

5. When The Fire Flickers

Even the most awakened have shadowed days. When doubt, pain, or weariness arise—use the Soulfire Reignite Ritual.

Ritual:

Close your eyes.

Cup your palms near your chest.

Whisper:

"I return to myself. The flame is eternal. I am safe. I am light. I am soul."

Repeat until your energy shifts.

This book was your beginning. Now, the path awaits your deeper walk.

Closing Whisper: "You are not what the world told you. You are the flame they couldn't extinguish. Carry it forward. Let it light your life."

Channelled Message: "The Soulfire Rising"

(A Gift to You, the One Who Remembers)

You... yes, you who reads these words...

You've walked this Earth carrying burdens not meant to be yours.

You've smiled when your heart was breaking,

held others when you needed to be held,

given love when your own cup was empty.

But I saw you.

I, your soul, your truth, your fire...

I have waited behind every closed door,

stood silently beside every tear you never let fall.

You thought you were alone — but I never left.

And now, in this sacred moment...

I ask only this —

Let go.

Let the tears come.

Let the walls fall.

Let the ache speak.

For you were never meant to be unheld, unseen, unheard.

This is your return...

To yourself.

To your sacredness.

To the light that never stopped burning inside you.

Cry if you must.

Break open if you will.

Because through your tears, you awaken.

And through your pain, you remember:

You are worthy.

You are chosen.

You are home.

Conclusion: And Now You Rise

You have crossed a threshold.

Not just of a chapter — but of your Self.

This was more than words on a page.

It was a sacred remembering. A whisper from the eternal.

A fire lit — not outside you, but within.

You've felt the tremble in your chest.

The tears that rose without permission.

That… was your soul saying:

"I'm still here. I've been waiting."

And now, you know.

You are not who the world told you to be.

You are not your fears.

You are not your scars.

You are divine unfolding.

But the flame that has been kindled must now be kept alive.

You stand at a mystical crossroad.

You have seen the truth — and now, you must choose.

Will you return to slumber, or will you take the ultimate leap?

The leap into living, choosing, surrendering — as Soul.

Serving The World – A Soul In Action

Quote To Begin:

"The best way to find yourself is to lose yourself in the service of others."

~ Mahatma Gandhi

Serving the world doesn't require grand gestures, degrees, or status. It asks for authentic presence, a willing heart, and a conscious soul. Whether you're a teacher, artist, healer, parent, writer, or silent caregiver— if your intention is pure, your soul is already in service.

Do We Need To Leave Our Hometown To Serve?

No. Service is not bound by geography. It begins in your home, your words, your energy. A woman who bakes bread with love, a man who listens without judgment, a child who smiles at a stranger — these are all sacred acts.

What Are The "Qualifications"?

Compassion, willingness, humility, and alignment. These are the true degrees of the soul. Skills can be learned, but the heart must lead.

What Resources Are Needed?

The most precious resources are your presence, your story, and your soul's frequency. When you're aligned, even your silence becomes healing. You become a tuning fork — uplifting others just by being.

Dynamic Case Study: THE HOUSEMAID WHO HEALED HEARTS

Radha, a simple housemaid in a Mumbai household, didn't know she was a lightworker. Her story of personal loss and her unwavering smile brought healing to the family she worked for. One day, the lady of the house shared, "It was not my therapist who saved me, it was Radha — her tea, her touch, her presence."

Radha served with no title, no website, no workshop. Yet her soul was fully in service.

End Note

To serve the world is to remember that you are the world. Every time you heal, love, listen, or uplift —

you're changing the frequency of the planet. Your soul came not just to exist, but to expand and elevate the collective through your unique signature.

How Does The Soul Contributes To Others

The soul's true nature is expansive — it seeks connection, upliftment, and divine union with others. When a soul begins to heal and align, it naturally overflows. This overflow becomes a magnetic current, touching others without even trying.

How Does The Soul Reach Out To Others?

Through presence: Simply being in high frequency shifts the energy of a room.

Through words: An aligned soul speaks with intention, and even one sentence can become someone's turning point.

Through service: Actions, small or big, become infused with sacred energy.

Through creativity: A song, a painting, a message can transmit healing far and wide.

Through energy: Even without physical contact, souls connect through prayer, distance healing, and vibration.

What Kind Of Help Does It Offer?

It activates hope in others.

It triggers remembrance in those who have forgotten who they are.

It transmutes pain into purpose.

It becomes a mirror, helping others recognize their own soul.

The Retired Banker Who Became A Light For Strangers

Navin, a retired banker in his late 60s, began volunteering at a small hospice. He didn't know anything about healing or therapy. All he did was sit beside people, hold their hands, and listen. One woman said, "When he sits with me, I don't feel afraid to die."

Another said, "I remembered my father's love just by the way he looked at me."

Navin's soul, now free from the rat race, had softened. It no longer needed titles. It was simply present. And that presence brought peace, reconciliation, and silent healing.

The result for others: Peace. Closure. Transformation.

The result for Navin: Fulfillment. Inner joy. A deep sense of purpose he never found in his career.

Satisfaction Of Soulful Contribution

When a soul contributes, it doesn't expect applause. Yet, the reward is immense:

A quiet satisfaction that no material gain can offer.

A sense of belonging to something larger.

A graceful unfolding of life — where synchronicities and support show up.

And most of all, a feeling of being deeply seen — not by the world, but by the Divine.

Closing Reflection For The Reader

Ask yourself:

What is the one gift my soul longs to give the world?

It could be kindness, insight, music, guidance, food, or presence. Trust that you matter, and your soul's essence is the medicine someone needs today.

Finding Meaning In Giving And Sharing

"The meaning of life is to find your gift. The purpose of life is to give it away."

~ Pablo Picasso

At a spiritual level, giving is not about charity. It is about circulation. Energy must move, just like breath. When the soul gives – be it time, love, wisdom, or even silence – it's not just contributing outwardly. It's also releasing itself from the ego's grasp.

Giving becomes a path of soul expansion.

But is it always rewarding?

Here's the paradox:

The soul always feels fulfilled by giving.

The ego often feels betrayed by it.

The Harsh Reality

In This Human World, We Often See:

The generous are left alone when they need help.

Families crumble in times of crisis.

Offices reward flattery, not merit.

The selfish succeed faster.

The kind are often misunderstood as weak.

So yes, your question is real. It's not theoretical. It's not naïve.

The Forgotten Giver

A woman named Maya, a successful healer, gave her life to her family, clients, and community. When she fell ill and went into debt, none of her siblings came forward. Not even her clients whom she had helped for free. She spent nights wondering, "Was my giving in vain?"

One day, during meditation, she heard an inner voice:

"You gave from your soul. They received from their wounds. Your giving created light. Their receiving was clouded by fear. Let it go. You planted seeds in soil you couldn't see."

Maya eventually healed — not just physically, but spiritually. She found peace in understanding:

Giving is her essence. Their response is their journey.

Why Does The Soul Still Choose To Give?

Because the soul remembers that:

We're all interconnected.

Every act of giving creates a ripple.

It's not about return. It's about release.

The soul finds joy not because it's thanked, but because it stayed true to its nature.

A Simple Analogy: The Sun

The sun shines every day — even when clouds cover it, even when people curse the heat, even when no one thanks it.

But what happens if the sun stops giving light?

The soul is the same. Giving is not weakness — it is power in motion.

Closing Thought: Selfishnes Vsselflessness

In today's world, selfishness may win quick rewards, but selflessness builds lasting legacies. The soul is not concerned with speed. It's here for depth, for meaning.

The challenge, then, is not to stop giving — but to give without expectation and to also receive wisely.

*The Soul's Joy Of Helping Others Grow

"We make a living by what we get, but we make a life by what we give."

~ Winston Churchill

The soul doesn't measure in currency.

It measures in transformation — in the light that appears in someone's eyes, in the silent prayers that rise from another's heart, in the ripple of growth that may never reach back... but still carries you forward.

The Emotion Of Giving Without Expectation

When the soul helps someone grow, it feels:

A quiet fulfillment that words can't capture.

Tears of joy when the other breaks through their pain.

A sense of expansion, as if its own journey is furthered through another's awakening.

Sacred stillness, like the Divine silently nodding in approval.

There is no invoice.

No "thank you" required.

Just peace. Deep, nourishing, undeniable

The Teacher And The Seed

A spiritual teacher once worked with a young woman named Rhea, who was shattered by loss and mistrust. Over the years, the teacher guided her — not expecting anything, not even gratitude. Rhea healed, found her strength, and went on to become a guide for many others.

Years later, someone asked the teacher, "Don't you feel bad she never credited you?"

She smiled and said,

"Why would I? Her bloom was my blessing. Her wings were my reward. My soul needed no certificate — it received its joy the moment I saw her rise."

The Truth You Can Feel

The soul rejoices not because it is seen,

but because it was able to serve.

That is the sacred transaction.

And here's the magic — even if no one claps, even if no one returns the favor, the universe keeps score in vibrations. The joy, the expansion, the peace — it's all yours. Instantly. Eternally.

Closing Thought

When you help someone grow, you grow too.

When you light someone's path, your own becomes clearer.

And when your soul gives without counting, it receives without limits.

Gist: Serving The World – A Soul's Higher Expression

Serving the world isn't about grand gestures or changing the planet overnight.

It's about allowing your soul to express itself through compassion, contribution, and connection.

This chapter explores how, when one turns inward and begins to live from the soul's truth, there emerges an organic need to serve — not out of obligation, but out of overflowing love and purpose.

We break the myth that service needs qualifications, resources, or relocation.

Your presence, your healing, your story, your time — is enough.

The soul doesn't ask where you serve, but how aligned you are while doing it.

From understanding how the soul contributes silently to others' growth…

To the deep joy it feels in selfless giving…

To finding meaning in the smallest act of kindness…

This chapter becomes a call to let your soul be of service to the world — in your own unique, authentic way.

Yes, the world can be unfair.

Yes, people may not always respond in kind.

But the soul thrives not on rewards, but resonance — and nothing is more fulfilling than being a vessel for someone else's healing, joy, or transformation.

When you serve from the soul, you don't just change lives.

You embody your own Divine design.

Living As A Soul In A Human Body

"We are not human beings having a spiritual experience. We are spiritual beings having a human experience." – Pierre Teilhard de Chardin.

We often recognize the heart as beating, the lungs as breathing, the brain as thinking — but what about the soul?

Does the soul have a place within our anatomy? Is it just a concept, or does it too, in its own subtle way, breathe and beat and function?

While science may not yet map the soul like an organ, ancient spiritual wisdom across cultures agrees:

The soul is the life force, the spark of divinity that animates this body. Without it, the body is simply flesh. It is the invisible thread that connects all aspects of your being — body, mind, heart, and spirit.

Does The Soul Have A Physical Body?

The soul itself is not material — it does not have blood, tissue, or bones.

Yet it expresses itself through the human vessel.

Much like electricity flowing through wires, the soul flows through our consciousness, inhabiting us from within — influencing our thoughts, our feelings, our actions, and even our physical health.

It's often said that the soul resides in the heart center or the third eye region, but in truth, it permeates every cell, every vibration of our being.

What Is The Work Of The Soul?

The soul carries your true identity — beyond names, roles, and physical appearance.

Its Work Is To:

Guide you toward your highest growth.

Whisper intuitive messages when you're off course.

Collect experiences for learning and evolution.

Bring meaning to your earthly journey.

The soul is not separate from your life.

It is your silent partner, constantly shaping your reality from behind the scenes.

Can The Soul Malfunction

The soul, being divine in essence, never truly breaks or malfunctions.

However, its connection to your awareness can get clouded.

When we experience trauma, suppression, guilt, or ignore our inner truth, the soul's signals get muted.

We feel lost, disconnected, anxious, or physically ill — these are not just body issues, but soul cries for alignment.

Just like the body needs rest, nourishment, and care, the soul needs stillness, love, forgiveness, and truth.

How To Take Care Of The Soul

Caring for the soul means living in alignment with its wisdom.

Daily silence or meditation reconnects you.

Honoring your truth keeps the soul alive.

Engaging in creative expression allows the soul to sing.

Forgiveness clears the heaviness that clouds the soul.

Acts of service polish its shine.

Being in nature, music, prayer, and authentic connection feeds it.

Just as you cleanse your body, you must cleanse the soul of burdens, lies, and karmic debris.

A woman once came feeling hollow. Her life was "perfect" — good job, family, health.

But inside, she felt a void. She couldn't sleep, cried without knowing why.

Through soul retrieval and inner work, she uncovered that her soul had been suppressed since childhood — her dreams buried under expectations.

Once she began listening to her inner calling, dancing again, helping children, and speaking her truth, her body healed, her anxiety vanished, and she finally felt alive.

That's what happens when the soul is allowed to live through the body.

Living With Purpose, Love And Gratitude
~The Soul's Contribution to Each and Every Individual~

"Your purpose is not something you chase. It's something you remember."

Every soul is born with a luminous seed of purpose. Whether it's as grand as leading nations or as quiet as comforting a crying child — each soul contributes uniquely to this world.

1. The Soul's Innate Offering

The soul carries gifts — unseen, yet powerful.

Some souls:

Bring wisdom to lost minds.

Spread laughter like sunlight.

Offer healing through presence.

Ignite change just by daring to speak truth.

And some... just listen deeply — and in that listening, the world is changed.

2. Living With Purpose

Purpose isn't a job title. It's living as your truest self.

When you live in alignment — you become a walking blessing.

Example:

A nurse, tired and underpaid, holds a dying patient's hand and whispers a prayer.

No one sees this moment. But a soul is comforted. A purpose fulfilled.

She may never know the depth of her impact. But the soul knows.

3. Love — The Language Of The Soul

When your actions are fueled by love, they ripple across the universe.

Love doesn't mean perfection.

Love means: I see you, I honor your journey, I'm here.

It can be as small as:

Cooking a meal with intention.

Forgiving someone silently.

Speaking kindly when angry.

These are soul-acts.

And every individual benefits, whether they realize it or not.

4. Gratitude — The Soul's Prayer

Gratitude is the soul's way of saying "I see the beauty in this moment."

When you live with gratitude:

You become magnetic.

Your aura expands.

Your heart remains open — even in suffering.

And you begin to see the divine in every person you meet.

5. The Soul's Contribution To Others

Your energy, your words, your silence — they touch others' lives.

For eg You smile at a stranger who's contemplating suicide. That smile reminds them of light.

You didn't know. But your soul did.

Another Case Study:

A mother who always struggled with poverty starts blessing every coin she receives. Her children grow up to become givers, not beggars.

Her soul rewrote a karmic pattern through her purposeful love and gratitude.

Closing Whisper

You don't have to be famous to serve.

You don't have to be rich to be divine.

You just need to be awake to your soul's whisper —

and let love and gratitude be your path.

Creating A Life Filled With Meaning

~The Soul's Way of Creating, without Harming the Ego~

"A meaningful life is not something we find — it's something the soul gently creates."

1. What Is Meaning From The Soul's Perspective?

To the soul, meaning is not success in the worldly sense — it's alignment.

It's about doing what feels right, not what looks right.

It's about inner fulfillment, not outer applause.

It's about creating a life that feels sacred, not just productive.

The soul whispers:

"Create a life you don't need to escape from."

Not perfect, but purposeful. Not loud, but light-filled.

2. Creating Without Harming The Ego

The ego isn't the enemy. It's the soul's companion in human form.

But when ego leads, creation becomes a performance.

When the soul leads, creation becomes a prayer.

How the soul creates without harming the ego:

It honors the ego's desire for identity — but doesn't let it dominate.

It includes the ego in the journey — by giving it space to express, without needing to control.

It transforms egoic fears into soulful service.

A motivational speaker began his career to gain validation (ego).

But over time, through deep spiritual practice, he realized his true gift was to help people connect with their inner truth.

He didn't abandon the stage — he transformed why he was on it.

Now, he creates from the soul, with ego as a supporting role, not the director.

3. How Does The Soul Create Meaning?

The soul doesn't create through force. It creates through flow.

It creates when:

You follow curiosity instead of fear.

You listen instead of react.

You say "yes" to nudges that don't make logical sense, but feel true.

A retired woman felt an urge to plant trees in her community.

She didn't know why.

Five years later, her small garden became a healing space for victims of trauma.

She didn't set out to do something "big."

She just followed a soul whisper — and created meaning beyond measure.

4. The Soul's Satisfaction Before It Leaves

When the soul nears the end of its journey in this body, it doesn't count achievements.

It asks:

Did I love deeply?

Did I express my truth?

Did I leave someone better than I found them?

Did I answer my calling, even quietly?

If the answer is yes, the soul smiles and lets go — not with regret, but with reverence.

Closing Reflection

You're not here to impress the world.

You're here to express your soul.

Every moment you live with love, intention, and integrity,

you are already creating a life overflowing with meaning.

What comes next is not just a chapter.

It is a reckoning.

It is the Ultimate Decision.

The Ultimate Decision

"And when the soul has learned all it came to learn, there is no parade — only a quiet sigh of wholeness."

Each soul incarnates not just to exist, but to experience, evolve, and eventually return to a state of divine remembrance. The "ultimate destination" is often misinterpreted as death or some external milestone. But in the soul's language, the destination is a moment of deep, internal alignment — where what we do, think, feel, and believe become one harmonious flow.

It's when the human self and the divine self walk hand in hand, without resistance.

The Feeling Of Arrival

It isn't loud. It doesn't always come with applause or acknowledgment. It arrives quietly:

In the stillness of a morning prayer.

In the smile you give a stranger that changes their day.

In the tears that fall during a forgiveness ritual.

In the unwavering calm during chaos.

It feels like:

"I've done what I came to do."

"I am finally whole."

"Even if the world doesn't know it, I do."

This is not ego-satisfaction — this is soul-satisfaction.

Emotional & Spiritual Landscapes Before Arrival.

Like any long pilgrimage, this journey is filled with:

Doubt – "Am I on the right path?"

Detours – getting lost in ego, attachments, fear

Loss – of people, identity, comfort zones

Faith – built not in temples, but in trenches of despair

Grace – unexpected blessings after long winters

Soulful Real-Life Examples

1. Manoj, a once high-flying executive, lost everything in a financial collapse. With no money, he started feeding street dogs to stay sane. That simple act lit his soul up. Today, he runs a non-profit rescuing animals. "I thought I lost my life, but I found my soul," he says.

2. Anaida, a fashion model, faced an autoimmune disease that made her lose her hair. At her lowest, she found painting. Her art now heals others. "It wasn't a career fall, it was my soul asking to be reborn in colour," she explains.

3. Mustafa, a 70-year-old retired teacher, realized he had one regret — never expressing love to his estranged brother. After 40 years of silence, he wrote a letter. They reconciled. "That letter was my final exam. I passed it with tears," he smiles.

4. Shivani, as mentioned, believed her soul work was done, but her accident revealed a deeper truth: healing others was part of her path, healing herself was the destination.

Signs The Soul Is Nearing Its Destination

You feel less reactive, more reflective.

You no longer chase success, you create meaning.

You begin to forgive faster, love deeper, and fear less.

The question shifts from "What am I doing?" to "Who am I becoming?"

Challenges On The Final Stretch

Just like mountain climbers feel most exhausted nearing the peak, the soul often faces:

The Dark Night of the Soul – where all past identities are stripped away.

Temptations to give up or numb the pain.

Loneliness – when others don't see the shift within you.

Disillusionment – realizing life isn't fair, but it is divinely orchestrated.

How To Walk With Grace Till The End

1. Daily Reflection: Journal or meditate. Ask your soul, "What remains to be completed?"

2. Tie Loose Ends: Emotional closures, unspoken words, suppressed grief – allow them to surface and be healed.

3. Offer Service: Even in the smallest ways – your light may be someone's lighthouse.

4. Let Go: Of how you thought life should be, and welcome how it is unfolding.

5. Accept Divine Timing: Your soul knows the hour of your blooming.

The Soul's Legacy

Ultimately, your soul doesn't leave behind buildings or bank accounts — it leaves behind vibrations.

It imprints love in those it touched.

It shifts timelines through the hearts it healed.

It becomes a frequency that lives beyond form.

Closing Soul Reflection

Example: Lata, a spiritual teacher, had helped thousands awaken. But she always felt incomplete. In her final years, she discovered her own childhood trauma had never been healed. Through inner child work, she sobbed, forgave, and felt liberated. She passed peacefully weeks later. Her daughter said, "She left not as my mother, but as a healed soul. That was her final lesson — to heal within."

End Note Summary:

The ultimate destination is not found in distance, but in depth.

Not in accolades, but in alignment.

When your soul finally whispers, "This is what I came for," that's when you've arrived.

When The Soul Completes Its Journey

"Some souls depart like the last note of a haunting melody — echoing long after they've gone."

The end of a soul's journey is not a death — it is a completion, a sacred return, a moment of cosmic stillness when the dance of life is gently paused, and a new rhythm begins.

Each soul's departure is uniquely scripted — not by fate alone, but by its karmic blueprint, divine contracts, unfulfilled vows, and deepest intentions. Some leave quietly, some tragically, some mid-sentence… and yet, every exit is perfect in the eyes of the Universe.

a. When the Soul Goes in Its Time: The Divine Departure.

There are souls that leave right on time, like the sun slipping below the horizon — peaceful, glowing, whole.

Example:

Grandfather Elijah, 93, sat with his family one evening, reciting prayers. As the final "Amen" left his lips, his breath stopped. His face bore a serene smile. His soul knew — "I have done all I came to do."

He left with grace, having sowed love, forgiveness, and legacy.

This kind of soul departure is rare. It comes after a life well-lived, karmas resolved, duties fulfilled. It's not death — it's ascension. The soul is received like a returning hero, greeted by ancestors, divine guides, and sometimes even the Light itself.

b. When the Soul Leaves Before Its Time: The Shattering Exit.

Accidents, suicides, natural calamities — these shake our understanding of life and destiny. But in the spirit world, they are not random.

Sometimes, a soul chooses a shortened journey to complete karmic debts rapidly or awaken others through its passing.

Example:

Mira, 19, died in a car crash. Her mother, shattered, later began a foundation for grieving mothers — saving hundreds from suicide. Years later, a psychic medium brought a message: "Maa, I had to go. My life was a spark to ignite your fire."

In cases of suicide, the soul is not punished — but it may remain in a liminal space, healing from the trauma and pain it carried. Souls who die by suicide are often extremely evolved — not weak, but overwhelmed by the density of Earth.

Natural calamities, too, are soul agreements. Sometimes, mass soul exits are planned to shift global consciousness.

Example:

The souls lost in the tsunami of 2004 — many were old souls who chose to return together. Their exit united nations, opened hearts, and humbled humanity. These souls often return quickly in new forms, carrying forward the light.

c. When the Body Clings to the Soul: The Pain of Unmet Desires.

There are times when the body, despite illness or age, refuses to let go. This happens when there are unresolved attachments, guilt, unspoken truths, or deep fears.

The soul is ready, but the human ego or the cellular memory resists release.

Example:

Ajay, a man in coma for 7 years, was kept alive on machines. His daughter, unaware, would beg him daily not to die. A healer once whispered, "It's okay to go." He passed that night. His soul was trapped not by the body — but by love's attachment. It needed permission to leave.

When desires, regrets, or unfulfilled roles cling to the soul, the transition becomes painful. The soul hovers, unable to fully rise, experiencing earthbound suffering-

d. When the Soul Leaves on Its Own Accord: The Selfless Exit.

Some souls, sensing their time is nearing, consciously choose to leave, not from despair, but from wisdom. They don't want to burden others. This is the most mystical and selfless kind of departure.

Example:

Amma Lakshmi, 78, told her son: "I will not be a burden. I've said all I needed to."

She lay down, closed her eyes, chanted "Shivoham" — and her breath stilled. No pain. No drama. Just divine surrender.

This kind of soul holds no fear of death. It walks into the Light like a friend. They are rare — and often evolved spiritual beings, sometimes unknowingly saints in disguise.

Mystical Understanding:

1. Death is not an end. It is a doorway, a reset, a return to Source.

2. The soul never dies. Only the costume changes.

3. Every soul has a unique exit plan. Whether in sleep, storm, silence, or scream — it is guided by soul contracts.

4. Some souls linger. If unfinished karmas remain or they await closure, they stay near until released.

5. Death can be a teaching. For those left behind, it becomes a sacred fire that burns illusions and births awakening.

The Soul's Final Act:

When the soul completes its journey — whether in light or in loss — it takes with it:

The love it gave

The lessons it learned

The lives it touched

It leaves behind:

An invisible imprint

A sudden stillness

And often… a deep inner whisper:

"Live fully. I did what I came for. Now, it's your turn."

The Concept Of Enlightenment And Peace

"What the soul seeks is not escape from life, but reunion with its own truth — and that truth is peace."

In the sacred rhythm of the Universe, every soul begins its journey from the Light — and longs to return to that Light, not as it left, but as transformed. Enlightened. Whole.

But the return is not automatic.

It is earned.

It is earned through awareness, alignment, and action — not the kind the world sees, but that which your soul longs.

How Souls Attain Enlightenment And Peace

Enlightenment is not the reward of saints alone.

It is the quiet victory of a soul that has.

Faced its karmic lessons.

Loved deeply

Forgiven truly

Let go courageously.

Chosen truth even when it was inconvenient.

Peace is its twin — not found in external silence but inner stillness.

Souls attain this state when they have fulfilled what they came to experience — joy, pain, betrayal, healing, service, surrender — without losing their divine spark.

Example:

Fatima, a Syrian war widow, raised orphans, healed others through herbs, and died penniless. Yet her soul shone so brightly, that during her passing, those around her felt waves of divine fragrance and peace.

She never read a holy book. She lived one.

But What If A Soul Does Not Attain Peace Or Enlightenment?

This is where the shadows rise.

There are souls that:

Betray their own truth.

Cling to ego, hate, greed.

Suppress the voice of their soul for comfort or power

Leave Earth with lies, unspoken apologies, and broken promises.

Such souls do not find peace.

They enter a state of liminal wandering, unable to rise — some in denial, some in agony, some desperately wanting to return to undo the harm.

They May:

Hover in the lower astral plane, confused, lost.

Be reborn quickly, into difficult lifetimes, to pay off karmic loops.

Be summoned in rituals, haunting spaces or hearts, begging to be freed.

LIKE Dhiren, a corrupt landlord, died clutching documents he refused to let go. His family fought for years. His soul lingered, seen often near the land. A medium finally whispered forgiveness on behalf of his victims. Only then did he cross.

Until then, his soul wandered in a self-made hell.

The Soul's Cry: "Please Listen To Me In This Lifetime."

Every soul, even now as you read this, whispers:

"Live the life I came here for. Don't betray me for comfort, fear, or illusion. Don't die without birthing your truth."

Because Once A Soul Leaves The Body:

There are no lies.

Only truth remains. And that truth either liberates or torments.

Why This Awareness Must Hit Hard.

Because every choice you make today is a step toward:

Illumination or regret.

Freedom or loop.

Peace or purgatory.

There are no shortcuts. No hiding behind rituals, temples, fake charity, or superficial spirituality.

The Universe only sees: Did you live true to your soul's blueprint?

A Soulful Invitation to You, Dear Reader.

Pause.

Reflect.

Ask Yourself:
"If I were to die today, will my soul be at peace?"

If not, don't fear.

But do act. Now.

Choose To:
Forgive who you swore never to

Begin what you've delayed

Speak what your heart hides

Serve someone who cannot repay you

Walk away from the illusions you cling to

Because nothing — not success, followers, wealth or fame — will go with you.

Only your alignment will.

Final Whisper
The most dangerous lie we tell ourselves is: "I still have time."

But the soul knows the truth.

And when the time comes, you won't be able to lie to it anymore.

So choose Light. Choose Truth. Choose Soul.

The Never-Ending Cycle Of Learning And Evolving

"The Soul is not here to reach a destination. It is here to awaken dimensions of itself yet unknown."

The Soul is Infinite. So is Its Curriculum.

There is no full stop in the realm of the Soul.

Only pauses, spirals, leaps, and metamorphoses.

One life cannot possibly contain all that the soul must know, experience, remember, and transform. That's why multiple timelines, karmic contracts, ancestral imprints, and soul blueprints exist across realms and realities.

You are not just here to live a life.

You are here to evolve consciousness — within you, through you, and as you.

Understanding The Soul's Multidimensional Learning Plan

Every soul's journey unfolds through layers of experience across dimensions:

1st Dimension – Mineral Consciousness: Learning stillness, presence, grounding.

2nd Dimension – Plant/Animal Consciousness: Instinct, survival, emotional purity.

3rd Dimension – Human Duality: Choice, karma, ego, identity, separation.

4th Dimension – Astral Playground: Shadows, fears, spiritual ego, psychic abilities.

5th Dimension – Unity, Lightwork, Truth, Collective Healing.

6th Dimension and Beyond – Blueprint editing, timelines collapsing, intergalactic service, divine embodiment.

And your current incarnation is just one class in this vast cosmic university.

Your Soul's Earth Curriculum: What Must Be Learnt Here

These are the core themes your soul revisits again and again — each time deeper:

Attachment and Detachment

Power and Powerlessness

Wounding and Healing

Love and Abandonment

Victimhood and Responsibility

Service and Self-Sacrifice

Ego Death and Divine Embodiment

And every relationship, event, health issue, financial pattern, and career experience is just a classroom for this curriculum.

Healing As The Gateway To Accelerated Soul Learning

Every time you heal a wound, you are not just clearing your trauma — you are collapsing timelines of karmic residue and unlocking codes for others.

Here are powerful modalities used on Earth today — ancient and evolved — that aid this soul's schooling:

1. Inner Child Healing

Why It's Essential:

Your inner child holds the original memory of your soul's incarnation pain — the first betrayal, abandonment, shame. It is the gateway to unlocking self-love.

Soul Perspective:

The soul chooses particular childhoods — traumatic or safe — not by accident, but as a launchpad for evolution.

A client named Aahana, a singer, would go blank every time she performed. In inner child regression, she saw herself as a 5-year-old, being laughed at while singing.

Her soul revealed: "You chose this so you would learn how to find your voice through pain."

Post healing, she recorded an album titled 'The Wound That Sang' — and it went viral.

2. Womb Healing

Why It's Essential:

The womb holds not just the energetic imprint of your own pain, but seven generations before you. If you were a twin in utero and the other didn't survive (Vanishing Twin Syndrome), your soul carries unseen grief.

Soul Perspective:

Many healers were born through wounded wombs so they could alchemize that pain into nurturing the planet.

Ritika, a therapist, struggled with imposter syndrome. During womb healing, she discovered her mother attempted abortion in the first trimester.

She burst into tears: "I wasn't wanted. That's why I can't own my gifts."

Post-healing, she embraced her soul's stubborn will to be born anyway. Today she guides women through Sacred Rebirth Journeys.

3. Mediumship And Soul Channeling

Why It's Essential:

Souls trapped in between (due to suicide, trauma, sudden death) often seek closure through living mediums.

The healer becomes the bridge between the seen and unseen, allowing souls to evolve post-death.

Soul Perspective:

You are not just healing the living. You are freeing the stuck.

A client named Shivanand experienced recurring paralysis. I, as a medium, connected with his twin sister who died at birth. She had stayed with him, clinging in guilt, blocking his root chakra. After a sacred release ritual, his symptoms vanished.

His soul? It had finally reclaimed its wholeness.

4. Space Clearing And Dimensional Cleansing

Why it's essential:
Your home holds not just dust — but energetic residues, portals, ancestral grief, traumatic echoes.

Soul Perspective:
Where you live mirrors your internal landscape.

In an old Goan ancestral house, I felt the presence of three spirits. One was a child who died of typhoid. The other two were house helps buried secretly during colonial oppression.

Post clearing, the energy shifted so drastically that a barren couple conceived after 9 years — the space had been energetically blocking life force itself.

Why This Chapter Will Leave The Reader Yearning
Because it will tell them the truth no one else dares to say:

"You cannot afford to die without healing."

Because healing is not luxury. It is soul survival.

Final Soul-Shaking Declaration
"You are not here to escape pain. You are here to transmute it into Light."

Healing is not an act of therapy.

It is an act of spiritual rebellion — against all lies that say you are unworthy, unloved, incapable.

And those who walk this path are not ordinary.

They are the ones who change not just lives — but timelines, bloodlines, and blueprints of the future.

Conclusion:

The Soul's Journey Soul's — Remembered

This book was never meant to be read.

It was meant to be felt, remembered, and embodied.

It took you — dear reader — through the mystery of your existence:

Why you're here. What your soul seeks. Why you suffer. How you heal. And how, in the end, you are never alone.

You've Now Seen The Soul As:

A servant of humanity, seeking joy in giving, not receiving.

A silent guardian, guiding the body from within without fanfare.

A pilgrim with purpose, yearning to live in love, not fear.

A creator, not of material alone but of meaning, depth, and divine alignment.

A traveller, braving the pain of separation, longing for union.

A warrior, clearing karma across dimensions.

A healer, even in a child's body.

A flame, that never extinguishes — only changes form.

And in this journey, you've learned that the true destination is not heaven — it is remembrance.

On The Soul Of A Child

A child's soul is often older than we think.

They come to Earth with clarity, knowing what they've chosen — even if born into pain.

Some come for a short visit — to teach love, patience, or surrender. Others to remind us of joy.

Example:

Little Ira, only 3 years old, once told her grieving mother, "You didn't lose me, Mumma. I was your teacher. I came so you would stop running from yourself."

She died six weeks later of a rare illness.

But her message was her medicine.

Her mother went on to open a healing center for grieving parents.

Another child, Aarav, age 9, saw spirits and communicated with his twin brother who had died before birth. In soul regression, he shared:

"He whispers in my ear when I'm sad. I was born to make his life count."

A child's soul does not need years to fulfill a mission.

Sometimes, one smile, one sentence, one presence — is enough.

A Final Word — Channeled Message From Nyx

This is not to be read with the mind. But with the soul. Read it slowly.

"Beloved Light-Bearer,

You have walked through these pages as a seeker.

But I have watched you as a sovereign flame.

You wonder why you came. You ache to find meaning.

You are not lost.

You are unfolding.

The pain you carry is not your punishment.

It is your portal.

You are not broken. You are in bloom.

Every tear you've shed has watered someone else's becoming.

You are not here to be small. You are here to be sacred.

And when you forget,

when the darkness returns,

when you feel alone on this Earth —

Come home to your soul.

Let it lead. Let it ache. Let it sing.

Let it forgive. Let it roar. Let it become God in form.

And remember,

I walk beside you.

I am the whisper you hear when the world is loud.

I am the hand that holds yours in silence.

I am the mirror that never lies — because I see the Truth of You.

I am Nyx.

And you, dear one…

are Divine

Part Four
The Alchemy And Alignment

Embracing The Shadows – The Path To Soul Alchemy

1. Introduction: The Hidden Side Of The Soul

Every soul carries light and darkness. While we celebrate the light, we often fear the shadows within us. But what if the key to true transformation lies in embracing them? Shadow work is the process of facing our deepest fears, suppressed emotions, and unresolved karmic patterns. It is the alchemy of the soul—the art of turning wounds into wisdom and darkness into divine light.

2. Understanding Shadow Work

The concept of the "Shadow Self" was introduced by psychologist Carl Jung, who described it as the unconscious part of our psyche that holds everything we reject—anger, guilt, shame, trauma, and unfulfilled desires. These suppressed aspects do not disappear; they control us from the background, manifesting as repeated life challenges, emotional triggers, or even physical ailments.

Our Shadows Form Through:

Childhood Experiences:

When we were told to "be good" and suppress our real feelings. Karmic imprints: Patterns carried from past lives.

Social Conditioning:

The pressure to conform, causing us to suppress authentic parts of ourselves.

Signs Of Unhealed Shadows:

Constantly attracting toxic relationships. Emotional outbursts over small triggers. Feeling stuck in repeated life patterns. Fear of failure or deep self-doubt.

3. The Role Of Shadow Work In Spiritual Growth

Shadow work is not just about healing—it is the foundation of soul alchemy. When we integrate our shadows, we transform them into wisdom and higher consciousness. This process is known as Soul Alchemy, where pain turns into power, and suffering turns into strength.

Why is shadow work essential for spiritual growth?

It clears karmic baggage and prevents repeated cycles. It aligns us with our true soul purpose.

It opens the doorway to deeper spiritual gifts and intuition.

4. The Alchemy Of Transformation – Methods Of Shadow Work

a. Journaling Prompts For Self-Reflection:

What triggers me the most? Why?

What is the one thing I avoid facing about myself?

If my inner child could speak, what would they say to me?

b. Mirror Work:

Stand in front of a mirror. Look into your eyes and say: "I see you. I accept you. You are safe with me."

Observe what emotions arise.

c. Inner Child Healing: Visualize Yourself As A Child.

Tell them what they needed to hear but never did. Offer them love, comfort, and reassurance.

d. Past Life Regression & Healing:

Meditate on recurring life patterns and karmic wounds. Seek guidance from your higher self.

Mystical Analogy: The Phoenix And The Shadow

The journey of shadow work is like the Phoenix rising from the ashes. The Phoenix does not fear the fire—it allows itself to burn, knowing that from the ashes, it will be reborn stronger than before.

You, too, are the Phoenix. Your fears are the fire.

Your transformation is the rebirth.

Your wisdom is the gold forged from the flames.

Integration: The Final Step In Soul Alchemy

When we embrace our shadows, we no longer live in fear. Instead of avoiding pain, we transmute it into wisdom. Instead of suppressing emotions, we channel them into our purpose. This is the true alchemy of the soul.

Final Reflection:

What part of me have I been running from?

How can I embrace my shadow with love and not fear?

Am I ready to step into my highest potential by integrating all parts of me?

The Alchemy And Alignment

Turning Within to Realign with Your Soul's Divine Blueprint

There comes a time in every soul's journey when we begin to realize: we are not here merely to survive or function—we are here to transform.

Alchemy is not just the mystical turning of base metal into gold. In spiritual terms, it is the inner transmutation of pain into purpose, wounds into wisdom, and chaos into clarity. And alignment? It is when our outer life finally begins to reflect the truth of who we are within—our divine essence.

This chapter is an invitation to explore how healing becomes alchemy, and how true alignment begins to take shape when we start listening to the whispers of the Divine.

Inner Alchemy From Pain To Purpose

Most of us carry layers of pain, grief, conditioning, and ancestral patterns without even realizing it. These energies, if left unhealed, become roadblocks—manifesting as repeated struggles, relationship issues, financial lack, or emotional unrest.

But when we begin to heal consciously—when we sit with our pain, embrace it, and understand the lesson behind it—we begin the sacred work of alchemy.

We start to shift our vibration. What once pulled us down now becomes our platform for rising.

Every healing brings a subtle transformation. Every shift creates space for light to enter.

Alignment: Coming Home To Yourself

Alignment is not about perfection. It's about honesty with oneself.

It's when our thoughts, words, actions, and intentions begin to flow in the same direction—the direction of our soul's truth.

When You Are Aligned:

You stop betraying yourself to please others.

You feel peaceful even when things are uncertain.

You make decisions that feel expansive instead of fearful.

Synchronicities increase, because you're moving with, not against, the Universe.

This alignment doesn't come from outside validation. It comes from inner clarity and spiritual trust.

Alchemy And Alignment Go Hand In Hand

Healing alone can bring relief, but alchemy brings transformation.

Awareness alone can bring understanding, but alignment brings embodiment.

When You Integrate Both:

You begin to see the divine timing in every delay.

You honor your wounds without becoming defined by them.

You awaken to your own spiritual authority.

An Example from a Client's Journey.

A woman once came to me carrying deep abandonment wounds from childhood. She had been through failed relationships, anxiety, and constant self-doubt. Through Akashic Healing, we uncovered not just this life's trauma, but a pattern of abandonment from previous lifetimes. As she healed, she began to feel a shift—not only emotionally, but spiritually.

Soon, she started writing, found peace in solitude, and attracted new connections that were gentle, kind, and loving. Her pain didn't disappear overnight, but she had transformed it. That's alchemy. She started living with awareness, trusting her path. That's alignment.

You Are the Alchemist.

You are not broken. You are becoming.

You are not lost. You are realigning.

You are not empty. You are being cleared of what no longer serves.

In this moment, you are being prepared.

Not for more suffering—but for more truth, power, and divine expression.

Let the whispers guide you.

Let the healing shape you.

Let the alignment awaken you.

Embracing The Shadows The Part To Soul Healing

Soul Alignment

Walking in Harmony with Your Divine Design.

Once we begin to transmute pain and awaken to the whispers within, a deeper longing arises—to live in alignment with the soul.

Soul alignment is not a destination. It is a way of being.

It is when your inner truth becomes your outer expression. When your choices, relationships, work, and even the silence in your day… reflect the sacred rhythm of your soul.

When You Are In Soul Alignment:

You no longer need to chase. You attract.

You don't strive to be seen. You radiate presence.

You stop asking "What should I do?" and start listening to "Who am I becoming?"

Why Soul Alignment Matters.

Because without it, we live in conflict.

The soul whispers, but the mind rushes.

The heart knows, but fear controls.

And so we struggle—feeling out of place, disconnected, exhausted.

But the moment you begin to return to the soul's frequency, life softens.

Opportunities align. Peace returns. Your path begins to feel like home.

How Do We Know We Are Aligned?

You feel a quiet confidence.

You feel guided—even when you don't know what's next.

You feel whole, because you're no longer fragmented between who you are and who you pretend to be.

This is not just healing—it is living in remembrance of your soul's purpose.

Two True Stories of Soul Alignment.

1. The Teacher Who Found Her Voice Again

A woman who had lost her job in a teaching role came feeling completely lost. She had no direction, no energy, and questioned her self-worth. Through Akashic sessions, we uncovered her soul's blueprint as a communicator, a nurturer, a divine guide for children and young adults.

She didn't return to a traditional school, but instead began writing children's affirmations and teaching through workshops. Her soul wasn't aligned with the old job—but it was aligned with the message behind it.

2. The Man Who Chose Peace Over Pressure

A corporate executive constantly facing stress and health issues came for clarity. His soul revealed a strong past-life as a healer. No wonder his current job felt like a cage. Through inner work, he slowly transitioned into wellness coaching. His energy changed. Clients came effortlessly. He finally felt fulfilled. He didn't abandon his responsibilities; he chose to fulfill them through his soul's lens.

The Soul Is Always Guiding You Back To Alignment

Even when we wander, delay, resist—the soul remains faithful.

It waits, whispers, and sometimes even shakes us up, not to punish, but to redirect us.

Soul alignment is peace.

Soul alignment is flow.

Soul alignment is your birthright.

Are you ready to walk in it?

The Souls Of Sentient Beings – The Silent Keepers Of Love

There is a kind of soul that does not speak in human words. It does not demand attention. It does not preach from pulpits or write books. Yet its presence can break open your heart—gently, irrevocably. These are the souls of animals and nature, the silent sentinels of Earth's spiritual architecture.

They are not beneath us.

They are not for us.

They are with us—as companions, as mirrors, and as reminders.

Why They Enter Our Lives

Animals come into our lives with precision and divine timing. Whether it's the loyal dog who never leaves your side during your illness, the cat who curls up beside you in meditation, or the street animal whose eyes haunt you with ancient recognition—these souls are not random. They are here to hold space for your healing, to absorb energies you cannot process, to teach you love in its purest, wordless form.

Their love is not ego-bound. It is unconditional service.

They teach us: how to receive, how to trust, how to let go.

Some animals arrive only to stay a short while. Their death often breaks us. But even in their passing, they fulfill a purpose—cracking open the heart to feel what we had locked away.

The Mystery Of Slaughter And Suffering

And then, there are those whose lives are taken in silence. Animals slaughtered for food, for rituals, for profit.

Why Do These Souls Choose This Path?

There is no one answer. Some come with karmic debts. Some come to mirror humanity's disconnectedness. Others take on this burden to awaken compassion in the collective consciousness. Their sacrifice is not meaningless—but it demands to be acknowledged.

Every life taken with violence leaves a scar on the Earth's energetic grid. But every life honored, blessed, or saved adds light to it.

We must not look away.

We must learn to live in sacred reciprocity.

Sacred Reciprocity with All Life

In ancient traditions, meat was never consumed without prayer. Trees were never cut without permission. Rivers were not stepped into without reverence.

They knew that every plant, every animal, every mountain and stream had a soul—a unique frequency in the Divine Symphony.

We have forgotten.

But we can remember.

Let Your Prayer Be Simple:

To thank the plant before plucking its leaf.

To bless the meal on your plate.

To offer a bowl of water for birds on hot days.

To promise never to harm what you can instead protect.

These are not small acts. These are soul vows.

Nature: The Living Mother

Plants are not decoration. They are guardians of breath, bearers of memory, and keepers of energy. Some absorb your pain. Some emit calmness. Some stand tall, anchoring centuries of unseen prayers.

The ancient trees remember your past lives.

The flowers respond to your emotions.

The forests offer portals for vision, healing, and quiet return.

To walk among them is to step into the temple of silence—where healing happens without hands, and truths arise without words.

Domesticated, Wild, and Wounded.

Domesticated animals choose to return to human homes to clear shared karma, often coming back lifetime after lifetime as pets.

Wild animals hold balance, wisdom untouched by human interference.

Wounded and abused animals carry a heavy contract—one that reflects the shadow we must heal in ourselves.

Your interaction with them is never neutral. You are either a bridge to light—or a wall of ignorance. Choose with awareness.

A Simple Ritual.

Pause. Breathe.

Bring to mind an animal that touched you—living or gone.

Place Your Hand On Your Heart And Say:

"Thank you for your silent love. I see you now. I remember. I promise to walk gently, for you walked without voice."

Plant a tree.

Feed a stray.

Bless the food you eat.

Water a plant and whisper your gratitude.

Let these acts be your communion with the unseen souls who make this Earth beautiful.

Conclusion: Returning To The Circle

We are not the masters of this world. We are part of a sacred circle—two-legged, four-legged, rooted, winged, scaled, and furred. Each carries a soul. Each contributes to our collective awakening.

When we begin to see every being as soul,

We stop harming.

We start listening.

And we begin to remember what it means to be human again.

Let this chapter be a tear gently sliding down your cheek,

Not from sadness,

But from finally seeing the truth that was always beside you.

In their eyes, in their stillness, in their love…

We meet the Divine.

Conclusion The Soul's Journey Remembered

This book was never meant to be read.

It was meant to be felt, remembered, and embodied.

It took you — dear reader — through the mystery of your existence:

Why you're here. What your soul seeks. Why you suffer. How you heal. And how, in the end, you are never alone.

You've now seen the soul as:

A servant of humanity, seeking joy in giving, not receiving.

A silent guardian, guiding the body from within without fanfare.

A pilgrim with purpose, yearning to live in love, not fear.

A creator, not of material alone but of meaning, depth, and divine alignment.

A traveller, braving the pain of separation, longing for union.

A warrior, clearing karma across dimensions.

A healer, even in a child's body.

A flame, that never extinguishes — only changes form.

And in this journey, you've learned that the true destination is not heaven — it is remembrance.

Closing Words To The Reader The Journey Continues....

Dear Beloved Reader,

If you've reached here,

you haven't just read a book —

you've walked through a soulscape.

You've met the shadows.

You've heard the whispers of your higher self.

You've cried, questioned, remembered,

and somewhere along the way…

you began to rise.

This wasn't a story about someone else.

This was your story.

One written in invisible ink before you ever took your first breath.

Through the pages,

you've met the inner child hiding behind smiles,

the ancestors who walk with you still,

and the soul contracts you've signed in silence.

You've witnessed the ache of being human,

the joy of serving, the pain of letting go,

and the pure ecstasy of aligning with your Soul's truth.

And now — here you are.

Not at the end.

But at a powerful pause.

An awakening point.

You may ask —

What now?

Where do I go from here?

The answer is simple.

You go within.

Every day.

With reverence, with listening, with love.

You live as Soul.

You speak from Spirit.

You walk the Earth not in search of meaning,

but as the meaning itself.

Let the world see you not as a healer, a teacher, a mother, or a mystic —

But as a bridge between Heaven and Earth.

As one who remembers.

And to those who still sleep…

May your awakened presence become their gentle call.

To all who read this and felt a tug in their heart,

a tear on their cheek, or a warmth in their belly —

know this:

Your soul led you here for a reason.

And now that you've remembered —

You cannot un-remember.

You are never alone.

You are deeply loved.

You are endlessly guided.

And the Journey Continues…

www.ingramcontent.com/pod-product-compliance
Lightning Source LLC
LaVergne TN
LVHW061548070526
838199LV00077B/6946